HARPERCOLLINS COLLEGE OUTLINE

Introduction to Calculus

Joan Dykes, Ph.D.
Edison Community College

HarperPerennial
A Division of HarperCollins*Publishers*

An American BookWorks Corporation Production

Project Manager: William Hamill

Editor: Robert A. Weinstein

Library of Congress Catalog Card Number: 91-58268

ISBN: 0-06-467125-9

92 93 94 95 96 ABW/RRD 10 9 8 7 6 5 4 3 2 1

Contents

Preface

This book is provided as a supplement to a standard Calculus textbook. Although a knowledge of intermediate algebra and trigonometry is assumed, as many steps as possible are provided to help the reader follow the logic involved in solving the various types of problems encountered in a first semester Calculus course. Theorems are stated and without proof and are often restated in words or symbols more easily understood by my own students. A set of exercises and answers appear at the end of each chapter to allow the reader to practice and receive immediate feedback. Keep pencil and paper handy—reading and working through this book will help you succeed in calculus.

1

Introductory Topics

---

*T*his chapter contains a short review of some of the algebraic topics that will be encountered in the remainder of the book. We will review the real number system, interval notation, solving inequalities, and graphing in the Cartesian plane.

1.1 REAL NUMBERS, INEQUALITIES, AND ABSOLUTE VALUE

Real Numbers

Our study of calculus will involve the real numbers. The union of the set of rational numbers (numbers that can be written as a ratio of two integers) and the set of irrational numbers (numbers that cannot be written as a terminating or repeating decimal) is the set of real numbers. We use a number line to picture the real numbers:

Irrationals $-\sqrt{3}, \sqrt{2}, e, \pi$

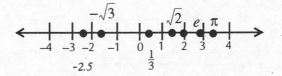

Rationals $-2.5, \frac{1}{3}, 2$

Order

We compare real numbers using the symbols

$<$ less than
$\leq$ less than or equal to
$>$ greater than

$\geq$ greater than or equal to

where $\frac{1}{3} < \sqrt{2}$ means $\frac{1}{3}$ lies to the left of $\sqrt{2}$ on the number line.

Interval Notation and Set Notation

We will often use subsets of the real numbers as solutions to equations or inequalities. These subsets are usually described with either interval notation or set notation as demonstrated in the following table.

Interval Notation	Set Notation	Graph
$(-1, 3)$	$\{x: -1 < x < 3\}$	open at -1, open at 3
$[-1, 3]$	$\{x: -1 \leq x \leq 3\}$	closed at -1, closed at 3
$(-1, 3]$	$\{x: -1 < x \leq 3\}$	open at -1, closed at 3
$[-1, 3)$	$\{x: -1 \leq x < 3\}$	closed at -1, open at 3

Notice that a parenthesis corresponds to an endpoint that is *not* included in the set (you may have graphed these as open dots in the past). A bracket corresponds to an endpoint that *is* included in the set (graphed as a closed dot in the past). The set notation "$\{x:$" is read "the set of all x such that."

EXAMPLE 1

Graph each set on a number line.

a) $(-2, 0)$

b) $[1, 3]$

c) $(-\sqrt{5}, 1]$

SOLUTION 1

a)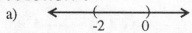

b)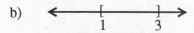

c)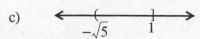

Notice that the endpoints on each graph match the endpoint notation for the intervals.

EXAMPLE 2

Write each set in interval notation and then graph each set
on a number line.

a) $\{x: \ 3 \le x \le 5\}$

b) $\{x: \ -1 < x < 2\}$

c) $\{x: \ -\sqrt{2} \le x < \sqrt{2}\}$

SOLUTION 2

a) $[3, 5]$ Since the endpoints are included in the solution, use brackets.

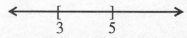

Endpoints on the graph match the interval notation.

b) $(-1, 2)$ Since the endpoints are *not* included in the solution, use parentheses.

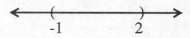

Endpoints on the graph match the interval notation.

c) $[-\sqrt{2}, \sqrt{2})$ Since $x \ge -\sqrt{2}$, use a bracket on the left. Since $x < \sqrt{2}$, use a parenthesis on the right.

Endpoints on the graph match the interval notation.

Unbounded
Intervals

    To represent unbounded sets of numbers we use the symbols ∞ (positive infinity) and $-\infty$ (negative infinity). The table below contains examples of unbounded intervals.

Interval Notation	Set Notation	Graph
$[2, \infty)$	$\{x: x \ge 2\}$	
$(-\infty, 1)$	$\{x: \ x < 1\}$	
$(-\infty, -1) \cup (3, \infty)$	$\{x: x < -1 \ \text{or} \ x > 3\}$	

Note that ∞ and $-\infty$ can *never* be included as endpoints

EXAMPLE 3

Complete the following table.

Interval Notation	Set Notation	Graph
$[-1, 4)$		
	$\{x: \ x \geq -1\}$	

SOLUTION 3

Interval Notation	Set Notation	Graph
$[-1, 4)$	$\{x: \ -1 \leq x < 4\}$	
$[-1, \infty)$	$\{x: x \geq -1\}$	
$(-\infty, 2)$	$\{x: \ x < 2\}$	

Solving First-degree and Compound Inequalities

We solve inequalities such as $2x - 5 < 7$ as though the $<$ were an $=$. Recall that the only exception occurs when we multiply or divide both sides of an inequality by a negative number, in which case we must reverse the inequality symbol. Compare the following solutions:

$2x - 5 < 7$ $\qquad\qquad\qquad\qquad$ $-2x - 5 < 7$

$2x - 5 + 5 < 7 + 5$ $\quad$ Add 5 to both sides $\quad$ $-2x - 5 + 5 < 7 + 5$

$2x < 12$ $\qquad\qquad$ Simplify. $\qquad\qquad$ $-2x < 12$

$\dfrac{2x}{2} < \dfrac{12}{2}$ $\qquad$ Divide by the $\qquad$ $\dfrac{-2x}{-2} < \dfrac{12}{-2}$

$\qquad\qquad\qquad\quad$ coefficient of x.

$x < 6$ $\qquad\qquad\qquad\qquad\qquad\qquad$ $x > -6$

$\qquad\quad$ Remember to reverse the inequality symbol.

EXAMPLE 4

Solve each inequality. Write the solutions using interval notation.

a) $3x - 2 \geq 5x + 6$

b) $-\dfrac{2}{3}x - 3 \le 5$

c) $-4 < 2x + 1 < 7$

SOLUTION 4

a) $3x - 2 + 2 \ge 5x + 6 + 2$ Add 2 to both sides.

    $3x \ge 5x + 8$ Simplify.

    $3x - 5x \ge 5x + 8 - 5x$ Subtract $5x$ from both sides.

    $-2x \ge 8$ Combine similar terms.

    $\dfrac{-2x}{-2} \le \dfrac{8}{-2}$ Divide both sides by -2. Reverse the inequality

    $x \le -4$ symbol.

    $x \le -4$ is written as $(-\infty, -4]$ in interval notation.

b) $-\dfrac{2}{3}x - 3 + 3 \le 5 + 3$ Add 3 to both sides.

    $-\dfrac{2}{3}x \le 8$ Simplify.

    $-\dfrac{3}{2}\left(-\dfrac{2}{3}x\right) \ge -\dfrac{3}{2}(8)$ Multiply both sides by $-\dfrac{3}{2}$. Reverse the inequality

    $x \ge -12$ symbol.

    $x \ge -12$ is written as $[-12, \infty)$ in interval notation.

c) $-4 < 2x + 1 < 7$

This inequality means $-4 < 2x + 1$ *and* $2x + 1 < 7$. We could solve each inequality separately, but as a shortcut, we'll solve this inequality by working on all three parts at the same time.

    $-4 - 1 < 2x + 1 - 1 < 7 - 1$ Subtract 1 from all three parts.

    $-5 < 2x < 6$ Combine similar terms.

    $-\dfrac{5}{2} < \dfrac{2x}{2} < \dfrac{6}{2}$ Divide all three parts by 2.

    $-\dfrac{5}{2} < x < 3$

    $-\dfrac{5}{2} < x < 3$ is written as $\left(-\dfrac{5}{2}, 3\right)$ in interval notation.

Absolute Value

The distance of a number a from zero is its **absolute value**, written $|a|$. For example, $|-3| = 3$, $|6| = 6$, $|0| = 0$. The following properties of absolute values will be used in this text:

Properties of Absolute Value

$|ab| = |a||b|$

$\left|\dfrac{a}{b}\right| = \dfrac{|a|}{|b|}, \ b \neq 0$

$|a| = \sqrt{a^2}$

$|a + b| \leq |a| + |b|$

$|x| = a$ if and only if $x = a$ or $x = -a$

$|x| < a$ if and only if $-a < x < a$

$|x| > a$ if and only if $x > a$ or $x < -a$

EXAMPLE 5

Solve. Write each solution in interval notation.

a) $|3x + 5| = 8$

b) $|4x - 1| < 7$

c) $|6 - 2x| \geq 6$

SOLUTION 5

a) $|3x + 5| = 8$ Given absolute value equation.

$3x + 5 = 8$ or $3x + 5 = -8$ Write the equivalent form without absolute value.

$3x + 5 - 5 = 8 - 5 \quad 3x + 5 - 5 = -8 - 5$ Solve each equation.

$\quad\quad 3x = 3 \quad\quad\quad\quad\quad 3x = -13$ Divide by 3.

$\quad\quad\quad x = 1 \quad\quad$ or $\quad\quad x = -\dfrac{13}{3}$

The solution set is $\{1, -\dfrac{13}{3}\}$. Since this solution consists of two points, *not* an interval, the answer cannot be written in interval notation.

b) $|4x - 1| < 7$ Given form of $|x| < a$.

$-7 < 4x - 1 < 7$ Write the equivalent form
without absolute value.

$-7 + 1 < 4x - 1 + 1 < 7 + 1$ Add 1 to all three parts.

$-6 < 4x < 8$ Combine similar terms.

$-\dfrac{6}{4} < \dfrac{4x}{4} < \dfrac{8}{4}$ Divide by 4.

$-\dfrac{3}{2} < x < 2$ Simplify.

$-\dfrac{3}{2} < x < 2$ is written as $(-\dfrac{3}{2}, 2)$ in interval notation.

c) $|6 - 2x| \geq 6$ Given form of $|x| \geq a$.

$6 - 2x \geq 6 \qquad$ or $\qquad 6 - 2x \leq -6$ Write the equivalent form
without absolute value.

$6 - 2x - 6 \geq 6 - 6 \quad 6 - 2x - 6 \leq -6 - 6$ Solve each inequality.

$-2x \geq 0 \qquad\qquad -2x \leq -12$

$\dfrac{-2x}{-2} \leq \dfrac{0}{-2} \qquad\qquad \dfrac{-2x}{-2} \geq \dfrac{-12}{-2}$ Divide by -2. Reverse the
inequality symbol.

$x \leq 0 \qquad$ or $\qquad x \geq 6$

$x \leq 0$ is written as $(-\infty, 0]$. $x \geq 6$ is written as $[6, \infty)$. Using $\cup$ for union (or), the solution set is written $(-\infty, 0] \cup [6, \infty)$.

Quadratic Inequalities

The technique we'll use to solve quadratic inequalities ($ax^2 + bx + c \ \square \ 0$, where the box contains <, >, ≤, or ≥) will also be used in our work with graphing functions. Don't just follow the rules - try to understand why this technique works.

To Solve Quadratic Inequalities
1. Isolate 0 on the right side of the inequality.
2. Replace the inequality symbol with an equal sign and solve the resulting equation by factoring.
3. Use the solutions from step 2 as split points on a number line.
4. Choose a number in each region created by the split points, substitute it into each factor, and record the resulting signs (+ or –) on the number line.
5. Use the sign rules for products to determine regions to be shaded for the solution. Use brackets on split points to be included in the solution (≤ or ≥). Use parentheses on split points that are not included in the solution (< or >).

Note that if the quadratic equation in step 2 does *not* factor, you can use the quadratic formula to find the split points.

The Quadratic Formula
The solutions to $ax^2 + bx + c = 0$, $a \neq 0$ are $x = \dfrac{-b \pm \sqrt{b^2 - 4ac}}{2a}$

It will be easier to substitute a number from each region into the original inequality, shading the region(s) that result in true statements, rather than to write factors and substitute into them (See Example 6c).

EXAMPLE 6

Solve each inequality and graph the solution on a number line.

a) $x^2 - x > 6$

b) $2x^2 \leq 5x + 3$

c) $4x^2 + 20x + 7 \geq 0$

SOLUTION 6

a) $x^2 - x > 6$ Given inequality.

     $x^2 - x - 6 > 0$ Isolate 0 by subtracting 6 from both sides.

$(x - 3)(x + 2) = 0$

Change > to = and solve to find the split points.

$x - 3 = 0$ or $x + 2 = 0$

Set each factor equal to 0.

$x = 3$ $x = -2$

These are the split points.

Use a number from each region, substitute into each factor, and record the resulting sign.

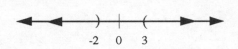

In Region I, $- \cdot - = +$

Use the sign rules for products to determine the sign for each region.

In Region II, $- \cdot + = -$

In Region III, $+ \cdot + = +$

We need positive answers since $x^2 - x - 6 > 0$ (greater than 0 implies positive), so our solution includes Region I and Region III:

Shade Regions I and III. Use parentheses on split points since they are not included in the solution.

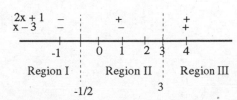

b) $2x^2 \leq 5x + 3$

Given inequality.

$2x^2 - 5x - 3 \leq 0$

Isolate 0.

$(2x + 1)(x - 3) = 0$

Change $\leq$ to = and solve to find the split points.

$2x + 1 = 0$ or $x - 3 = 0$

Set each factor equal to 0 and solve.

$2x = -1$

$x = -\dfrac{1}{2}$ $x = 3$

These are the split points.

Use a number from each region, substitute it into each factor, and record the resulting sign.

In Region I, $- \cdot - = +$

Use the sign rules for products to determine the sign for each region.

In Region II, $+ \cdot - = -$

In Region III, $+ \cdot + = +$

We need negative answers and answers equal to 0 since
$2x^2 - 5x - 3 \leq 0$, so our solution includes Region II and the split
points:

$\qquad$ -1/2 $\qquad$ 3

Shade Region II. Use
brackets on the split points
since they are included in
the solution.

c) $4x^2 + 20x + 7 \geq 0$ 0 is already isolated.

Since the quadratic equation $4x^2 + 20x + 7 = 0$ does not factor, we'll
use the quadratic formula:

$a = 4 \quad b = 20 \quad c = 7$ Identify a, b, and c.

$$x = \frac{-(20) \pm \sqrt{(20)^2 - 4(4)(7)}}{2(4)}$$

Substitute a, b, and c into

$$x = \frac{-b \pm \sqrt{b^2 - 4ac}}{2a}.$$

$$x = \frac{-20 \pm \sqrt{400 - 112}}{8}$$ Simplify the radicand.

$$x = \frac{-20 \pm \sqrt{288}}{8}$$ Simplify the radicand.

$$x = \frac{-20 \pm 12\sqrt{2}}{8}$$ $\sqrt{288} = \sqrt{144 \cdot 2} = 12\sqrt{2}$

$$x = \frac{4(-5 \pm 3\sqrt{2})}{8}$$ Factor the numerator.

$$x = \frac{-5 \pm 3\sqrt{2}}{2}$$ Reduce $\dfrac{4}{8} = \dfrac{1}{2}$.

$$\frac{-5 + 3\sqrt{2}}{2} \cong -0.4 \text{ or } \frac{-5 - 3\sqrt{2}}{2} \cong -4.6$$

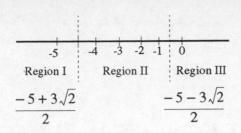

Use the split points and a number line to set up regions.

$$\frac{-5+3\sqrt{2}}{2} \qquad \frac{-5-3\sqrt{2}}{2}$$

Region I: Let $x = -5$

$4(-5)^2 + 20(-5) + 7 \overset{?}{\geq} 0$

$4(25) - 100 + 7 \overset{?}{\geq} 0$

$100 - 100 + 7 \overset{?}{\geq} 0$

$7 \geq 0$

Choose a number in Region I.
Substitute into the original inequality.
Simplify.

Simplify.
A true statement, so we include Region I in the solution.

Region II: Let $x = -1$

$4(-1)^2 + 20(-1) + 7 \overset{?}{\geq} 0$

$4(1) - 20 + 7 \overset{?}{\geq} 0$

$4 - 20 + 7 \overset{?}{\geq} 0$

$-9 \geq 0$

Choose a number in Region II.
Substitute into the original inequality.
Simplify.

A false statement, so we do *not* include Region II in the solution.

Region III: Let $x = 0$

$4(0)^2 + 20(0) + 7 \overset{?}{\geq} 0$

$7 \geq 0$

Choose a number in Region III.
Substitute into the original inequality.
A true statement, so we include Region III in the solution.

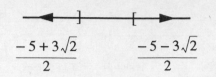

Shade Regions I and III.
Use brackets on the split
points

1.2 THE CARTESIAN PLANE

The Cartesian Plane

An **ordered pair** (x, y) consists of two numbers in a specific order in parentheses. The first number is called the **x-coordinate** or **abscissa**, and the second number is called the **y-coordinate** or **ordinate**.

We use a Cartesian plane consisting of two number lines at right angles. The horizontal number line is usually the *x*-axis, and the vertical number line is usually the *y*-axis. The axes meet at the **origin** (0, 0). The four regions formed by the axes are called **quadrants** and are labeled counterclockwise as shown below.

The ordered pair (2, 4) is graphed or plotted by locating the point where $x = 2$ and $y = 4$:

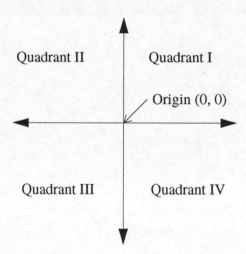

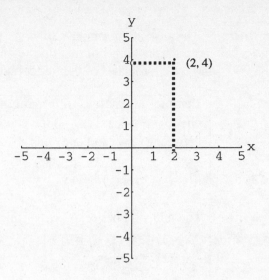

EXAMPLE 7

Plot the points (−2, 5), (−2, −3), (1, −4), (3, 0) and (0, −2) on the same set of axes.

SOLUTION 7

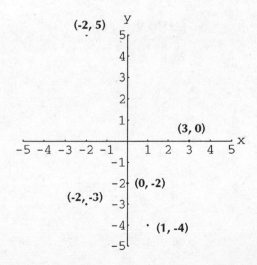

The Distance and Midpoint Formulas

The distance formula allows us to find the length of a line segment given the endpoints of that line segment. The midpoint formula is used to find the coordinates of the midpoint of a line segment.

Distance and Midpoint Formulas

Given (x_1, y_1) and (x_2, y_2) the endpoints of a line segment, the distance between (x_1, y_1) and (x_2, y_2) is

$$d = \sqrt{(x_2 - x_1)^2 + (y_2 - y_1)^2}$$

The midpoint between (x_1, y_1) and (x_2, y_2) is

$$M = \left(\frac{x_1 + x_2}{2}, \frac{y_1 + y_2}{2} \right)$$

EXAMPLE 8

Find the distance between the points and the midpoint of the line segment joining the points.

a) $(3, -1)$ and $(-3, 4)$

b) $(\sqrt{2}, 2)$ and $(-3\sqrt{2}, -5)$

SOLUTION 8

a)   Let $(x_1, y_1) = (3, -1)$ and $(x_2, y_2) = (-3, 4)$.

$$d = \sqrt{(x_2 - x_1)^2 + (y_2 - y_1)^2}$$ Write the distance formula.

$$d = \sqrt{(-3 - 3)^2 + (4 - (-1))^2}$$ Substitute $x_1 = 3$, $y_1 = -1$, $x_2 = -3$, $y_2 = 4$.

$$d = \sqrt{(-6)^2 + (5)^2}$$ Simplify inside parentheses.

$$d = \sqrt{36 + 25}$$ Simplify under the square root.

$$d = \sqrt{61}$$ Add.

$$M = (\frac{x_1 + x_2}{2}, \frac{y_1 + y_2}{2})$$ Write the midpoint formula.

$$M = (\frac{3 + (-3)}{2}, \frac{-1 + 4}{2})$$

Substitute $x_1 = 3$, $y_1 = -1$,
$x_2 = -3$, $y_2 = 4$.

$$M = (\frac{0}{2}, \frac{3}{2})$$

Simplify.

$$M = (0, \frac{3}{2})$$

b) Let $(x_1, y_1) = (\sqrt{2}, 2)$ and $(x_2, y_2) = (-3\sqrt{2}, -5)$

$$d = \sqrt{(x_2 - x_1)^2 + (y_2 - y_1)^2}$$

Write the distance formula.

$$d = \sqrt{(-3\sqrt{2} - \sqrt{2})^2 + (-5 - 2)^2}$$

Substitute $x_1 = \sqrt{2}$, $y_1 = 2$,
$x_2 = -3\sqrt{2}$, $y_2 = -5$.

$$d = \sqrt{(-4\sqrt{2})^2 + (-7)^2}$$

Simplify inside the
parentheses.

$$d = \sqrt{32 + 49} \, (-4\sqrt{2})^2$$

$$= (-4\sqrt{2})(-4\sqrt{2}) = 16\sqrt{4} = 32$$

$$d = \sqrt{81}$$

Add.

$$d = 9$$

Simplify the square root.

$$M = (\frac{x_1 + x_2}{2}, \frac{y_1 + y_2}{2})$$

Write the midpoint formula.

$$M = (\frac{\sqrt{2} + (-3\sqrt{2})}{2}, \frac{2 + (-5)}{2})$$

Substitute $x_1 = \sqrt{2}$, $y_1 = 2$,
$x_2 = -3\sqrt{2}$, $y_2 = -5$.

$$M = (\frac{-2\sqrt{2}}{2}, -\frac{3}{2})$$

Simplify.

$$M = (-\sqrt{2}, -\frac{3}{2})$$

Reduce.

Note in Example 8 that we could have chosen either ordered pair to represent (x_1, y_1). Try Example 8a) on your own, letting $(x_1, y_1) = (-3, 4)$ and $(x_2, y_2) = (3, -1)$.

Circles

A **circle** is the set of all points in a plane that are equally distant from a given point called the **center**. The distance from the center to a point on the circle is called the **radius**. The **diameter** of a circle is a line segment with endpoints on the circle and passing through the center of the circle.

> **Equation of a Circle**
> The standard form of the equation of a circle with center (h, k) and radius r is $(x - h)^2 + (y - k)^2 = r^2$.

Finding the Equation of a Circle

If we know (or can find) the center of a circle and its radius, we can use the standard form of the equation of a circle to write an equation that represents that circle. Notice that the coordinates of the center are *subtracted* from x and y in the standard form.

EXAMPLE 9

Write the equation of each circle in standard form.

a)   Center $(2, 3)$ and radius 4.

b)   Center at the origin and radius 1.

c)   Center $(-1, -2)$ and radius 3.

d)   Endpoints of a diameter: $(-2, 2)$, $(-6, -2)$.

SOLUTION 9

a) $(h, k) = (2, 3)$ $r = 4$ — Identify h, k, and r.

$(x - h)^2 + (y - k)^2 = r^2$ — Write the standard form of the equation of a circle.

$(x - 2)^2 + (y - 3)^2 = 4^2$ — Substitute for h, k, and r.

$(x - 2)^2 + (y - 3)^2 = 16$ — Simplify.

b) $(h, k) = (0, 0)$ $r = 1$ — Center at the origin means $(h, k) = (0, 0)$.

$(x - h)^2 + (y - k)^2 = r^2$ — Write the standard form of the equation of a circle.

$(x - 0)^2 + (y - 0)^2 = 1^2$ — Substitute for h, k, and r.

$x^2 + y^2 = 1$ — Simplify.

Note that a circle with center (0, 0) and radius 1 is called a **unit circle**.

c) $(h, k) = (-1, -2)$ $r = 3$ Identify h, k, and r.

$(x - h)^2 + (y - k)^2 = r^2$ Write the standard form of the equation of a circle.

$(x - (-1))^2 + (y - (-2))^2 = 3^2$ Substitute for h, k, and r.

$(x + 1)^2 + (y + 2)^2 = 9$ Simplify.

d) The center of a circle is the midpoint of a diameter of the circle. By finding the midpoint of the segment from $(-2, 2)$ to $(-6, -2)$, we'll find the center of the circle.

Let $(x_1, y_1) = (-2, 2)$ and $(x_2, y_2) = (-6, -2)$

$$M = \left(\frac{x_1 + x_2}{2}, \frac{y_1 + y_2}{2} \right)$$ Write the formula for the midpoint.

$$M = (\frac{-2 - 6}{2}, \frac{2 - 2}{2})$$ Substitute.

$$M = (-\frac{8}{2}, \frac{0}{2})$$ Simplify.

$$M = (-4, 0)$$ Simplify.

Since the radius is the distance from the center to any point on the circle, we'll find the distance from the center $(-4, 0)$ to $(-2, 2)$.

$$d = \sqrt{(x_2 - x_1)^2 + (y_2 - y_1)^2}$$ Write the distance formula.

$$d = \sqrt{(-4 - (-2))^2 + (0 - 2)^2}$$ Substitute.

$$d = \sqrt{(-2)^2 + (-2)^2}$$ Simplify.

$$d = \sqrt{4 + 4}$$

$$d = \sqrt{8}$$

$(h, k) = (-4, 0)$ $r = \sqrt{8}$ Identify h, k, and r.

$(x - h)^2 + (y - k)^2 = r^2$ Write the standard form of the equation of a circle.

$(x - (-4))^2 + (y - 0)^2 = (\sqrt{8})^2$ Substitute for h, k, and r.

$$(x+4)^2 + y^2 = 8 \qquad\qquad \text{Simplify.}$$

Finding the Center and Radius

When the equation of a circle is written in standard form, we can read the center and radius from the equation. However, often the equation of a circle will be given in **general form**:

$$Ax^2 + Ay^2 + Cx + Dy + F = 0, \ A \neq 0$$

We use completing the square to convert from general form to standard form. To complete the square, divide both sides of the equation by the coefficient of x^2, and then add (1/2 times the coefficient of x)^2 and (1/2 times the coefficient of y)^2 to both sides.

EXAMPLE 10

Find the center and radius of each circle.

a) $x^2 + y^2 - 4x + 2y - 4 = 0$

b) $2x^2 + 2y^2 + 12y + 10 = 0$

SOLUTION 10

a) $(x^2 - 4x \quad) + (y^2 + 2y \quad) = 4$ Group the x^2 and x terms, y^2 and y terms and add 4 to both sides.

$(x^2 - 4x + 4) + (y^2 + 2y + 1) = 4 + 4 + 1$ $\left(\dfrac{1}{2} \cdot -4\right)^2 = (-2)^2 = 4$

$\left(\dfrac{1}{2} \cdot 2\right)^2 = (1)^2 = 1$

$(x - 2)^2 + (y + 1)^2 = 9$ Factor.

$(x - 2)^2 + (y - (-1))^2 = 3^2$ Write in the form $(x - h)^2 + (y - k)^2 = r^2$

The center is at $(2, -1)$ and the radius is 3.

b) $2x^2 + 2y^2 + 12y + 10 = 0$

$x^2 + y^2 + 6y + 5 = 0$ Divide by 2.

$x^2 + (y^2 + 6y \quad) = -5$ Group the y^2 and y term and subtract 5 from both sides.

$x^2 + (y^2 + 6y + 9) = -5 + 9$ $\left(\dfrac{1}{2} \cdot 6\right)^2 = (3)^2 = 9$

$$x^2 + (y + 3)^2 = 4 \qquad \text{Factor.}$$
$$(x - 0)^2 + (y - (-3))^2 = 2^2 \qquad \text{Write in the form}$$
$$(x - h)^2 + (y - k)^2 = r^2.$$

The center is at $(0, -3)$ and the radius is 2.

1.3 LINES

There are many formulas associated with linear equations, some of which are presented in the following table. These formulas should be memorized.

Name	Formula	Notes
slope of a line	$m = \dfrac{y_2 - y_1}{x_2 - x_1}$	Also $\dfrac{rise}{run}$. (x_1, y_1) and (x_2, y_2) represent any two points on the line.
standard form of a line	$Ax + By = C$	The constant is isolated.
general form of a line	$Ax + By + C = 0$	Zero is on the right side.
point-slope form of a line	$y - y_1 = m(x - x_1)$	Replace y_1, m, and x_1.
slope-intercept form of a line	$y = mx + b$	Replace m and b, where b is the y intercept.
vertical line through (a, b)	$x = a$	Vertical lines have undefined slope.
horizontal line through (a, b)	$y = b$	Horizontal lines have 0 slope.

Slope

Given two points on a line, we find slope using $m = \dfrac{y_2 - y_1}{x_2 - x_1}$. Given an equation of a line, we find slope by first writing the equation in $y = mx + b$ form. In this form, the coefficient of x is the slope, m.

EXAMPLE 11

Find the slope of the line.

a) passing through $(5, -1)$ and $(-6, -3)$

b) $y = \dfrac{2}{3}x + 6$

c) $2x - 5y = 10$

SOLUTION 11

a) Let $(x_1, y_1) = (5, -1)$ and $(x_2, y_2) = (-6, -3)$

$$m = \frac{y_2 - y_1}{x_2 - x_1}$$

Write the formula for slope.

$$m = \frac{-3 - (-1)}{-6 - 5}$$

Substitute.

$$m = \frac{-2}{-11} = \frac{2}{11}$$

Simplify.

b) $y = \dfrac{2}{3}x + 6$

The line is already in $y = mx + b$ form.

$$m = \frac{2}{3}$$

Slope is the coefficient of x.

c) $2x - 5y = 10$

Write the equation in $y = mx + b$ form.

$-5y = -2x + 10$

Isolate y.

$y = \dfrac{2}{5}x - 2$

Divide by -5.

$$m = \frac{2}{5}$$

Slope is the coefficient of x.

Writing Equations of Lines

The table below will help you decide when to use each form of a linear equation.

Given This Data	Use This Form	Name of the Form
Slope m and y-intercept b	$y = mx + b$	Slope-intercept
Point (x_1, y_1) and slope m	$y - y_1 = m(x - x_1)$	Point-slope
Two points (x_1, y_1) and (x_2, y_2)	First find $$m = \frac{y_2 - y_1}{x_2 - x_1}$$ and then use: $y - y_1 = m(x - x_1)$	Slope Point-slope
Vertical line through (a,b)	$x = a$	
Horizontal line through (a,b)	$y = b$	

EXAMPLE 12

Write the equation of the line using the given information.

a) $m = \dfrac{3}{4}$, containing the point $(0, 2)$

b) containing the points $(5, -1)$ and $(-6, -3)$

c) m undefined, containing the point $(-1, 4)$

d) $m = 0$, containing the point $(2, -6)$

SOLUTION 12

a) Note that in the ordered pair $(0, 2)$, 2 is the y-intercept, b.

$y = mx + b$ Use the slope-intercept form.

$$y = \frac{3}{4}x + 2$$ Substitute $m = \frac{3}{4}$, $b = 2$.

If you had not recognized (0, 2) as the y-intercept, you could use the point-slope formula:

$(x_1, y_1) = (0, 2)$, $m = \frac{3}{4}$

$y - y_1 = m(x - x_1)$ Write the point-slope form.

$$y - 2 = \frac{3}{4}(x - 0)$$ Substitute.

$$y - 2 = \frac{3}{4}x$$ Simplify.

$$y = \frac{3}{4}x + 2$$ Same solution.

b) Let $(x_1, y_1) = (5, -1)$ and $(x_2, y_2) = (-6, -3)$

$$m = \frac{y_2 - y_1}{x_2 - x_1} = \frac{2}{11}$$ Find m (see Example 11a).

Then use:

$y - y_1 = m(x - x_1)$ Write the point-slope form.

$$y - (-1) = \frac{2}{11}(x - 5)$$ Substitute.

$$y + 1 = \frac{2}{11}x - \frac{10}{11}$$ Simplify.

$$y = \frac{2}{11}x - \frac{21}{11}$$ Answer is written in slope-intercept form.

c) m undefined means this is a vertical line.

$x = a$ Write the form for a vertical line.

$x = -1$ $(a, b) = (-1, 4)$

d) $m = 0$ means this is a horizontal line.

$y = b$ Write the form for a horizontal line.

$y = -6$ $(a, b) = (2, -6)$

Parallel and Perpendicular Lines

Recall from geometry that parallel lines are distinct lines in the same plane that do not intersect. Perpendicular lines are lines in the same plane that intersect at right angles. The slopes of parallel and perpendicular lines are related as follows.

> **Slopes of Parallel and Perpendicular Lines**
> Parallel lines have equal slopes.
> Perpendicular lines have slopes that are negative reciprocals of each other(a and $-1/a$, for $a \neq 0$).

EXAMPLE 13

Find an equation of the line

a) containing $(\frac{1}{2}, \frac{3}{4})$ and parallel to $2x - 3y = 6$

b) containing $(-1, -3)$ and perpendicular to $x = 4$

SOLUTION 13

a) Find the slope of $2x - 3y = 6$:

$$-3y = -2x + 6 \qquad\qquad \text{Isolate } y.$$
$$y = \frac{2}{3}x - 2 \qquad\qquad \text{Divide by } -3.$$

$m = \frac{2}{3}$, and any line parallel to this line has slope $m = \frac{2}{3}$.

$$(x_1, y_1) = (\frac{1}{2}, \frac{3}{4}) \quad m = \frac{2}{3}$$

$$y - y_1 = m(x - x_1) \qquad\qquad \text{Write the point-slope form.}$$

$$y - \frac{3}{4} = \frac{2}{3}(x - \frac{1}{2}) \qquad\qquad \text{Substitute.}$$

$$y - \frac{3}{4} = \frac{2}{3}x - \frac{1}{3} \qquad\qquad \text{Simplify.}$$

$$y = \frac{2}{3}x + \frac{5}{12} \qquad -\frac{1}{3} + \frac{3}{4} = -\frac{4}{12} + \frac{9}{12} = \frac{5}{12}$$

b) Note that $x = 4$ is a vertical line, and any line perpendicular to it must be a horizontal line.

$$y = b$$ Write the form for a horizontal line.

$$y = -3$$ $(a,b) = (-1, -3)$.

1.4 GRAPHING EQUATIONS

Graphing by Plotting Points

Probably your first encounter with graphing involved a table of values, where you substituted *x*-values into a given equation, found *y*-values and then plotted those points. That method is still useful, especially when you don't recognize the type of equation. If you have plotted several points and still cannot connect them with a smooth curve, *plot more points*.

EXAMPLE 14

Graph.

a) $y = x^2 - 4$

b) $y = \sqrt{3 - x}$

SOLUTION 14

a) $y = x^2 - 4$

Let's complete the table:

x	y
-3	
-2	
-1	
0	
1	
2	
3	

If $x = -3$, $y = (-3)^2 - 4 = 9 - 4 = 5$
If $x = -2$, $y = (-2)^2 - 4 = 4 - 4 = 0$
If $x = -1$, $y = (-1)^2 - 4 = 1 - 4 = -3$
If $x = 0$, $y = (0)^2 - 4 = 0 - 4 = -4$
If $x = 1$, $y = (1)^2 - 4 = 1 - 4 = -3$
If $x = 2$, $y = (2)^2 - 4 = 4 - 4 = 0$
If $x = 3$, $y = (3)^2 - 4 = 9 - 4 = 5$

The table becomes:

x	y
-3	5
-2	0
-1	-3
0	-4
1	-3
2	0
3	5

Plot the points and connect with a smooth curve:

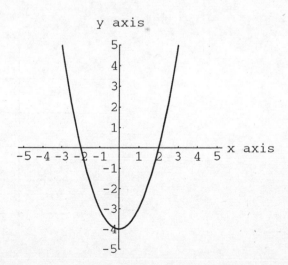

b) $y = \sqrt{3-x}$ Let's complete the table:

x	y
−3	
−2	
−1	
0	
1	
2	
3	

If $x = -3$, $y = \sqrt{3-(-3)} = \sqrt{3+3} = \sqrt{6}$

If $x = -2$, $y = \sqrt{3-(-2)} = \sqrt{3+2} = \sqrt{5}$

If $x = -1$, $y = \sqrt{3-(-1)} = \sqrt{3+1} = 2$

If $x = 0$, $y = \sqrt{3-(0)} = \sqrt{3}$

If $x = 1$, $y = \sqrt{3-(1)} = \sqrt{2}$

If $x = 2$, $y = \sqrt{3-(2)} = \sqrt{1} = 1$

If $x = 3$, $y = \sqrt{3-(3)} = \sqrt{0} = 0$

The table becomes:

x	y
−3	$\sqrt{6}$
−2	$\sqrt{5}$
−1	2
0	$\sqrt{3}$
1	$\sqrt{2}$

x	y
2	1
3	0

Plot the points and connect with a smooth curve:

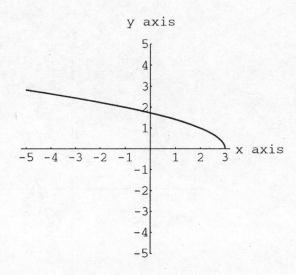

Graphing Lines and Circles

Although a table of values can be used to graph anything, we can graph lines and circles using their features.

> **Graphing Lines Using $y = mx + b$**
>
> 1. Put a point on the y-axis at the y-intercept b.
>
> 2. From b, use $m = \dfrac{rise}{run}$ to locate a second point on the line.
>
> 3. Draw a line through the two points.

EXAMPLE 15

Graph each line.
a) $y = 3x - 4$

b) $3x + 4y = 8$

SOLUTION 15

a) $y = 3x - 4$ The equation is already

written in $y = mx + b$ form.

$$m = 3 = \frac{3}{1} \quad b = -4$$ Identify m and b.

Start at $(0, -4)$. $m = \dfrac{3}{1} = \dfrac{rise}{run}$, so rise 3 units and run 1 unit:

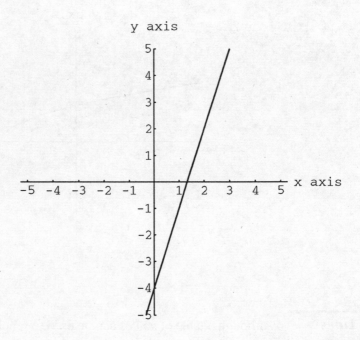

b) $3x + 4y = 8$ Write the equation in

$y = mx + b$ form.

$4y = -3x + 8$ Subtract $3x$ from both sides.

$$y = -\frac{3}{4}x + 2$$ Divide by 4.

$$m = \frac{-3}{4}, b = 2$$ Identify m and b.

Start at $(0, 2)$. $m = \dfrac{-3}{4}$ so fall 3 units and run 4 units:

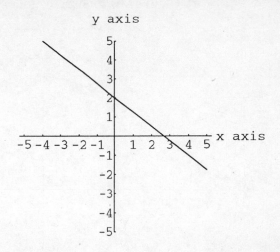

If we know the center and radius of a circle, we can plot the center and the four points that are horizontally and vertically a distance of *r* from the center.

EXAMPLE 16

Graph.

a) $x^2 + y^2 = 9$

b) $(x-2)^2 + (y+1)^2 = 16$

SOLUTION 16

a) $x^2 + y^2 = 9$ is a circle with center $(0, 0)$ and radius $r = 3$. Plot the center, and the points $(3, 0)$, $(0, 3)$, $(-3, 0)$, and $(0, -3)$.

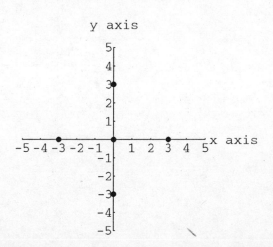

Now connect the four points on the circle (the center is *not* a point on the circle).

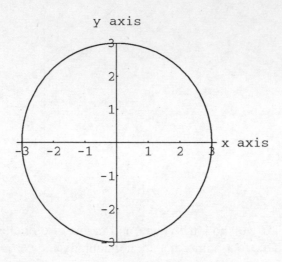

b) $(x-2)^2 + (y+1)^2 = 16$ is a circle with center $(2, -1)$ and radius $r = 4$. Plot the center, and the four points that are 4 units away horizontally and vertically:

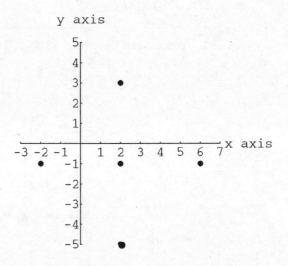

Now connect the four points on the circle:

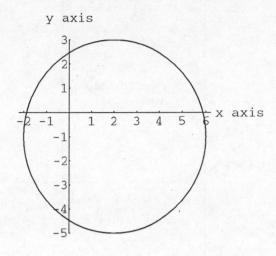

Symmetry

One of the aids used in graphing is symmetry. If we know a graph is symmetric with respect to the *y*-axis, origin, or *x*-axis, our table of values can be limited and the remainder of the graph is sketched using symmetry. Study the table that follows.

Type of Symmetry	Test	Graph
Symmetry with respect to the *y*-axis	Replacing *x* with −*x* yields an equivalent equation	Graph folds onto itself if folded along the *y*-axis

Type of Symmetry	Test	Graph
Symmetry with respect to the *x*-axis	Replacing *y* with −*y* yields an equivalent equation	Graph folds onto itself if folded along the *x*-axis
Symmetry with respect to the origin	Replacing *x* with −*x* and *y* with −*y* yields an equivalent equation	Graph folds onto itself if folded along the *x*-axis then the *y*-axis.

EXAMPLE 17

Determine whether the graph is symmetric with respect to the *y*-axis, *x*-axis, origin or none of these.

a) $x^2 + y^2 = 4$

b) $y = 4x^4 - 2x^2$

c) $x = 4y^2 - 1$

d) $y = 2x + 3$

SOLUTION 17

a) $x^2 + y^2 = 4$ Given equation.

    Test for symmetry with respect to the *y*-axis:

      $(-x)^2 + y^2 = 4$ Replace *x* with −*x*.

      $x^2 + y^2 = 4$ Equivalent equation.

    Therefore this graph is symmetric with respect to the *y*-axis.

Test for symmetry with respect to the *x*-axis:

$x^2 + (-y)^2 = 4$ Replace *y* with –*y*.

$x^2 + y^2 = 4$ Equivalent equation.

Therefore this graph is symmetric with respect to the *x*-axis.

Test for symmetry with respect to the origin:

$(-x)^2 + (-y)^2 = 4$ Replace *x* with –*x* and *y* with –*y*.

$x^2 + y^2 = 4$ Equivalent equation.

Therefore this graph is symmetric with respect to the origin.

b) $y = 4x^4 - 2x^2$

Test for symmetry with respect to the *y*-axis:

$y = 4(-x)^4 - 2(-x)^2$ Replace *x* with –*x*.

$y = 4x^4 - 2x^2$ Equivalent equation.

Therefore this graph is symmetric with respect to the *y*-axis.

Test for symmetry with respect to the *x*-axis:

$(-y) = 4x^4 - 2x^2$ Replace *y* with –*y*.

$y = -4x^4 + 2x^2$ *Not* an equivalent equation.

Therefore this graph is *not* symmetric with respect to the *x*-axis.

Test for symmetry with respect to the origin:

$(-y) = 4(-x)^4 - 2(-x)^2$ Replace *x* with –*x* and *y* with –*y*.

$-y = 4x^4 - 2x^2$ Simplify.

$y = -4x^4 + 2x^2$ *Not* an equivalent equation.

Therefore this graph is *not* symmetric with respect to the origin.

c) $x = 4y^2 - 1$

Test for symmetry with respect to the *y*-axis:

$(-x) = 4y^2$ Replace *x* with –*x*.

$-x = 4y^2 - 1$ Simplify.

$x = -4y^2 + 1$ *Not* an equivalent equation.

Therefore this graph is *not* symmetric with respect to the *y*-axis.

Test for symmetry with respect to the *x*-axis:

$x = 4(-y)^2 - 1$ Replace *y* with –*y*.

$x = 4y^2 - 1$ An equivalent equation.

Therefore this graph is symmetric with respect to the *x*-axis.

Test for symmetry with respect to the origin:

$(-x) = 4(-y)^2 - 1$	Replace x with $-x$ and y with $-y$.
$-x = 4y^2 - 1$	Simplify.
$x = -4y^2 + 1$	*Not* an equivalent equation.

Therefore this graph is *not* symmetric with respect to the origin.

d) $y = 2x + 3$

Test for symmetry with respect to the y-axis:

$y = 2(-x) + 3$	Replace x with $-x$.
$y = -2x + 3$	Simplify.
$y = -2x + 3$	*Not* an equivalent equation.

Therefore this graph is *not* symmetric with respect to the y-axis.

Test for symmetry with respect to the x-axis:

$(-y) = 2x + 3$	Replace y with $-y$.
$-y = 2x + 3$	Simplify.
$y = -2x - 3$	*Not* an equivalent equation.

Therefore this graph is *not* symmetric with respect to the x-axis.

Test for symmetry with respect to the origin:

$(-y) = 2(-x) + 3$	Replace x with $-x$ and y with $-y$.
$-y = -2x + 3$	Simplify.
$y = 2x - 3$	*Not* an equivalent equation.

Therefore this graph is *not* symmetric with respect to the origin.

Note from this example that a graph may be symmetric with respect to no axes, one axis, or both axes.

EXAMPLE 18

Use symmetry to help graph the following equations.

a) $y = 2x^2 + 1$

b) $x = y^4 - 3$

SOLUTION 18

a) $y = 2x^2 + 1$ is symmetric with respect to the y-axis:

$y = 2(-x)^2 + 1$	Replace x with $-x$.
$y = 2x^2 + 1$	Equivalent equation.

Therefore, our table of values need only contain 0 and positive values for x:

x	y
0	0
1	
2	

If $x = 0$, $y = 2(0)^2 + 1 = 1$
If $x = 1$, $y = 2(1)^2 + 1 = 3$
If $x = 2$, $y = 2(2)^2 + 1 = 9$
The table becomes

x	y
0	1
1	3
2	9

Plot these points, and their reflections across the y-axis:

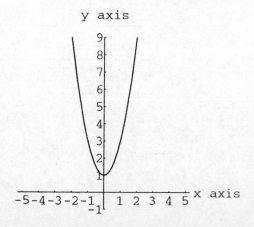

b) $x = y^4 - 3$

This graph is symmetric with respect to the x-axis:

$x = (-y)^4 - 3$ Replace y with $-y$.

$x = y^4 - 3$ Equivalent equation.

Therefore our table of values need only contain 0 and positive y values:

x	y
	0
	1
	2

If $y = 0$, $x = (0)^4 - 3 = -3$

If $y = 1$, $x = (1)^4 - 3 = -2$

If $y = 2$, $x = (2)^4 - 3 = 13$

Our table becomes

x	y
-3	0
-2	1
13	2

Plot these points and their reflections across the x-axis:

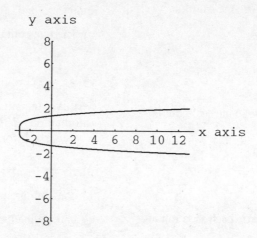

T*his chapter reviewed several important algebraic topics and formulas. A list of the formulas used in this chapter follows.*

The Quadratic Formula

$$x = \frac{-b \pm \sqrt{b^2 - 4ac}}{2a}$$

The Distance Formula

$$d = \sqrt{(x_2 - x_1)^2 + (y_2 - y_1)^2}$$

The Midpoint Formula

$$M = \left(\frac{x_1 + x_2}{2}, \frac{y_1 + y_2}{2}\right)$$

Equation of a Circle in Standard Form

$$(x - h)^2 + (y - k)^2 = r^2$$

Slope

$$m = \frac{y_2 - y_1}{x_2 - x_1}$$

Standard Form of a Line $Ax + By = C$

General Form of a Line $Ax + By + C = 0$

Point-Slope Form of a Line $y - y_1 = m(x - x_1)$

Slope-intercept Form of a Line $y = mx + b$

Practice Exercises

1. Solve each inequality. Write the solutions using interval notation.
   a) $2x - 5 \leq 5x + 7$
   b) $-\dfrac{1}{5}x + 4 > 1$
   c) $-1 < 3x - 4 < 1$

2. Solve. Write each solution in interval notation whenever possible.
   a) $|2x - 1| = 7$
   b) $|3x + 2| \leq 2$
   c) $|2 - 4x| > 6$

3. Solve each inequality. Write each solution in interval notation.
   a) $x^2 - x \leq 12$
   b) $3x^2 > -8x + 3$
   c) $x^2 + 14x + 9 \leq 0$

4. Find the distance between the given points.
   a) $(3, -6)$ and $(-7, -2)$
   b) $(2\sqrt{3}, -1)$ and $(5\sqrt{3}, 4)$

5. Find the midpoint of the line segment joining the points.
   a) $(2, -3)$ and $(-6, -1)$
   b) $(5, -3\sqrt{2})$ and $(-3, \sqrt{2})$

6. Write the equation of each circle in standard form.
   a) center $(-1, 3)$ and radius 2
   b) center at the origin and radius 5
   c) center $(-4, -1)$ and radius 4
   d) endpoints of a diameter: $(1, 0)$, $(1, -6)$

7. Find the center and radius of each circle.
   a) $x^2 + y^2 + 6x - 4y - 12 = 0$
   b) $3x^2 + 3y^2 - 24x - 6y - 24 = 0$

8. Find the slope of each line.
   a) The line containing $(6, -2)$ and $(-3, 4)$
   b) $y = -2x + 3$
   c) $4x - 3y = 6$

9. Write the equation of the line using the given information. Write each answer in $y = mx + b$ form whenever possible.
   a) $m = -\dfrac{2}{3}$, containing the point $(0, 1)$
   b) containing the points $(-2, 3)$ and $(1, -6)$
   c) m undefined, containing the point $(2, -1)$
   d) $m = 0$, containing the point $(-3, -4)$

10. Find an equation of the line
    a) containing $(\frac{2}{3}, -\frac{1}{2})$ and parallel to
       $3x + 2y = 4$
    b) containing $(2, -6)$ and perpendicular to
       $y = 3$.

11. Graph.
    a) $y = x^2 + 2$
    b) $y = \sqrt{x + 1}$
    c) $y = \dfrac{3}{2}x - 3$
    d) $2x + 5y = 10$
    e) $x^2 + y^2 = 25$
    f) $(x + 1)^2 + (y - 3)^2 = 16$

12. Determine whether each graph is symmetric with respect to the y-axis, the x-axis, the origin or none of these.
    a) $x^2 + y^2 = 1$
    b) $y = 3x^4 + x^2$
    c) $x = y^4 - 2$
    d) $y = x^3 - 2x^2 + 3x$

Answers

1. a) $[-4, \infty)$

    b) $(-\infty, 15)$

    c) $(1, \frac{5}{3})$

2. a) $\{-3, 4\}$
    b) $\left[-\frac{4}{3}, 0\right]$
    c) $(-\infty, -1) \cup (2, \infty)$

3. a) $[-3, 4]$
    b) $(-\infty, -3) \cup (\frac{1}{3}, \infty)$

    c) $[-7 - 2\sqrt{10}, -7 + 2\sqrt{10}]$

4. a) $2\sqrt{29}$
    b) $2\sqrt{13}$

5. a) $(-2, -2)$
    b) $(1, -\sqrt{2})$

6. a) $(x + 1)^2 + (y - 3)^2 = 4$
    b) $x^2 + y^2 = 25$
    c) $(x + 4)^2 + (y + 1)^2 = 16$
    d) $(x - 1)^2 + (y + 3)^2 = 9$

7. a) center $(-3, 2)$ $r = 5$
    b) center $(4, 1)$ $r = 5$

8. a) $-\frac{2}{3}$

    b) -2

    c) $\frac{4}{3}$

9. a) $y = -\frac{2}{3}x + 1$

    b) $y = -3x - 3$

    c) $x = 2$

    d) $y = -4$

10. a) $y = -\frac{3}{2}x + \frac{1}{2}$

    b) $x = 2$

11. a)

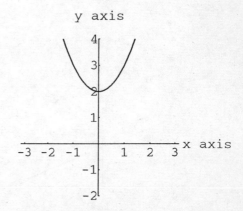

11. b)

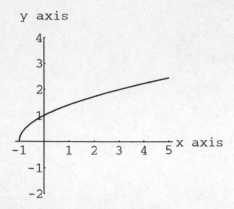

e)

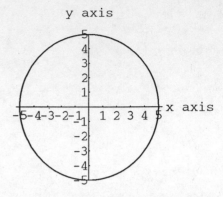

c)

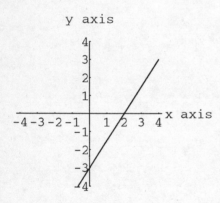

f)

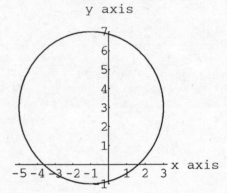

d)

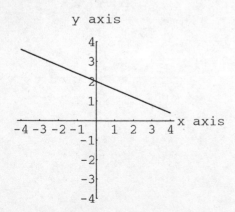

12. a) *y*-axis, *x*-axis and origin

b) *y*-axis

c) *x*-axis

d) none of these

2

Functions and Limits

*T*his chapter continues to review some precalculus topics including a review of functions and trigonometry. We then begin the first calculus topics of limits and continuity.

2.1 FUNCTIONS AND GRAPHS OF FUNCTIONS

The theorems and definitions in our study of calculus will involve functions. A thorough understanding of functions, function notation, and operations on functions is essential to your success.

A function is a set of ordered pairs in which no *x*-coordinate is repeated.

Study the following examples and counter examples.

Functions	Not Functions
$\{(0, 1), (2, 3), (3, 4)\}$	$\{(0, 1), (1, 2), (1, 3)\}$

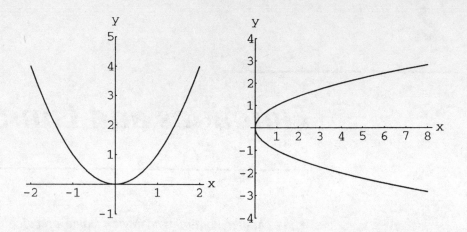

Notice in the counterexamples that an *x*-coordinate is repeated -- in the set of ordered pairs, 1 is paired with 2 and 3. In the graph, two points line up vertically, such as (4, 2) and (4, –2). This observation leads to the vertical line test.

The Vertical Line Test

If a vertical line can be drawn through more than one point on a graph, that graph does *not* represent a function.

EXAMPLE 1

Identify the functions.

a)

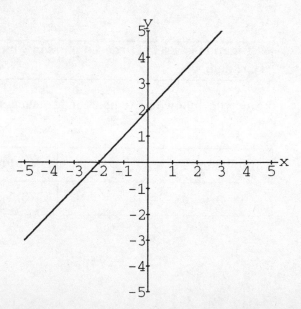

b)

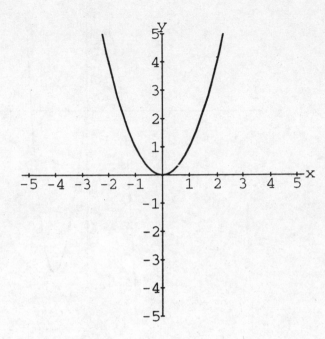

c)

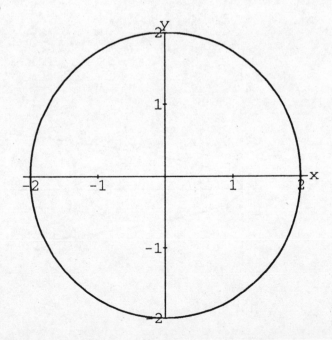

d)

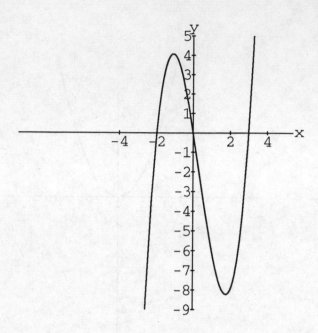

e)

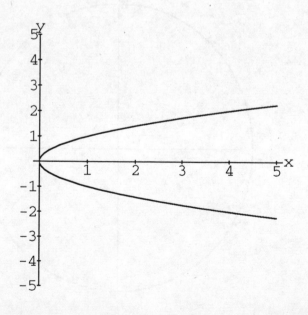

SOLUTION 1

a) Is a function.

b) Is a function.

c) Is not a function since a vertical line intersects the graph at more than one point.

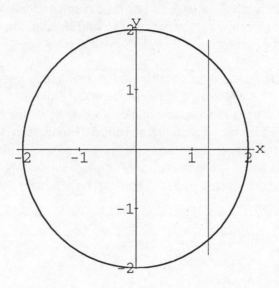

d) Is a function.

e) Is not a function since a vertical line intersects more than one point.

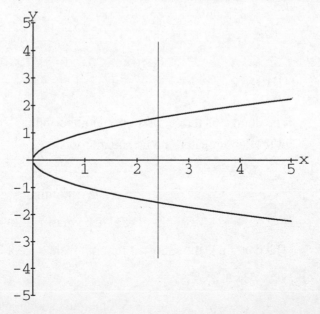

Domain and Range

Now that we can determine what represents a function, we return to the concept of domain (the set of x-coordinates) and range (the set of y-coordinates). If the domain of a function is *not* stated, it is assumed to be the largest set of real numbers which can be used as x values. Since we do not allow division by 0 or negative numbers under square root symbols, the following steps can be used to find the domain of a function when given an equation.

---

1. If there are no variables in the denominator or variables under a square root symbol, the domain is generally all real numbers.
2. If there is a variable in a denominator, set the denominator equal to 0 and solve. The domain is all real numbers *except* the values that make the denominator 0.
3. If there is a variable under a square root symbol, set the radicand greater than or equal to 0, and solve. The solution to the inequality is the domain.

EXAMPLE 2

Find the domain.

a) $y = 2x + 1$

b) $y = \dfrac{4}{x-2}$

c) $y = \sqrt{3x+2}$

d) $y = \dfrac{\sqrt{x-2}}{x-3}$

SOLUTION 2

a) $y = 2x + 1$

The domain is the set of all real numbers since there are no variables in the denominator and no square roots.

b) $y = \dfrac{4}{x-2}$

$x - 2 = 0$ Set the denominator equal to 0.

$x = 2$ Solve by adding 2 to both sides.

The domain is the set of all real numbers except 2.

c) $y = \sqrt{3x+2}$

$3x + 2 \geq 0$ Set the radicand greater than or equal to 0.

$$3x \geq -2 \qquad \text{Subtract 2 from both sides.}$$

$$x \geq -\frac{2}{3} \qquad \text{Divide by 3.}$$

The domain is the set of all real numbers greater than or equal to $-\frac{2}{3}$, written $\{x: x \geq -\frac{2}{3}\}$.

d) $y = \dfrac{\sqrt{x-2}}{x-3}$

$$x - 2 \geq 0 \qquad \text{Set the radicand greater than or equal to 0.}$$

$$x \geq 2 \qquad \text{Add 2 to both sides.}$$

$$x - 3 = 0 \qquad \text{Set the denominator equal to 0.}$$

$$x = 3 \qquad \text{Solve by adding 3 to both sides.}$$

The domain must contain x values that are greater than or equal to 2 *and not* equal to 3. Therefore, the domain is $\{x: x \geq 2, x \neq 3\}$.

Function Notation

In the past we have discussed the line $y = 2x + 1$, which we now know is a function. We use special notation for functions so that

$$y = 2x + 1 \quad \text{in function notation is} \quad f(x) = 2x + 1$$

$$y = x^2 \quad \text{in function notation is} \quad f(x) = x^2$$

$$y = \sqrt{x} \quad \text{in function notation is} \quad f(x) = \sqrt{x}$$

$f(x)$ is read "f of x", We often use lower case letters f, g, or h for functions. Thus, $g(x)$ would be read "g of x" (not g times x).

"Find $f(3)$" means find the value of the function (the y-coordinate) when $x = 3$. You are being asked to substitute 3 for x and simplify the results. For the function $f(x) = 2x^2 - x + 1$,

$$f(3) = 2(3)^2 - (3) + 1 \qquad \text{Substitute } x = 3.$$

$$= 2(9) - 3 + 1 \qquad \text{Simplify.}$$

$$= 16 \qquad \text{Add.}$$

EXAMPLE 3

If $g(x) = 3x^2 + 2x - 1$ find

a) $g(0)$

b) $g(-2)$

c) $g(*)$

d) $g(x + h)$

SOLUTION 3

a) $g(0) = 3(0)^2 + 2(0) - 1$ Substitute $x = 0$.

     $= 0 + 0 - 1$ Simplify.

     $= -1$

b) $g(-2) = 3(-2)^2 + 2(-2) - 1$ Substitute $x = -2$.

     $= 3(4) - 4 - 1$ Simplify exponents before multiplying.

     $= 12 - 4 - 1$ Multiply.

     $= 7$

c) $g(*) = 3(*)^2 + 2(*) - 1$ Substitute $x = *$.

d) $g(x + h) = 3(x + h)^2 + 2(x + h) - 1$ Substitute $x = x + h$.

$$(x + h)^2 = (x + h)(x + h)$$
$$= x^2 + 2xh + h^2$$

     $= 3x^2 + 6xh + 3h^2 + 2x + 2h - 1$ Use the distributive property.

Graphs of Functions   Several types of functions are used frequently in examples and exercises. Each of these graphs can be derived from a table of values. However, a familiarity with these graphs and the techniques for basic transformations will allow you to spend your time more productively.

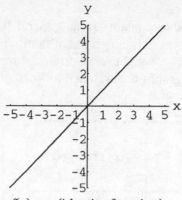

$f(x) = x$ (identity function)

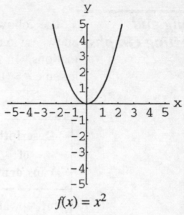

$f(x) = x^2$

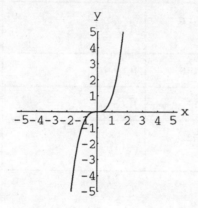

$f(x) = x^3$

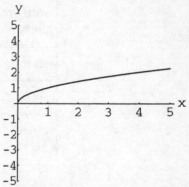

$f(x) = \sqrt{x}$

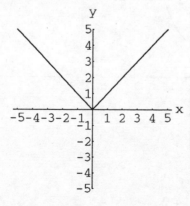

$f(x) = |x|$

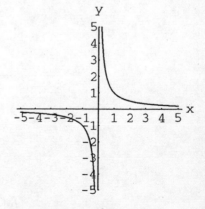

$f(x) = \dfrac{1}{x}$

Shifting and Reflecting Graphs

The following table contains some general transformations that will allow you to quickly sketch the graphs of familiar functions with transformations. In this table, we'll use an original function of $f(x) = x^2$ and assume $a > 0$. The graphs are sketched following the table.

Description of Transformation	$f(x)$ changed to:	Example
shift upward a units	$f(x) + a$	$f(x) = x^2 + 2$
shift downward a units	$f(x) - a$	$f(x) = x^2 - 1$
shift right a units	$f(x - a)$	$f(x) = (x - 2)^2$
shift left a units	$f(x + a)$	$f = (x + 1)^2$
reflect about the x-axis	$-f(x)$	$f(x) = -x^2$

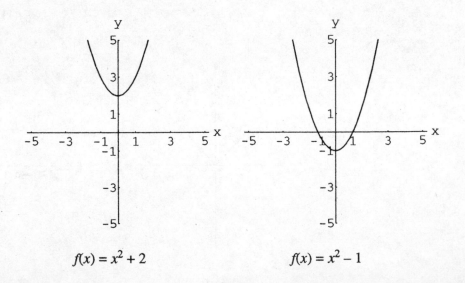

$$f(x) = x^2 + 2 \qquad f(x) = x^2 - 1$$

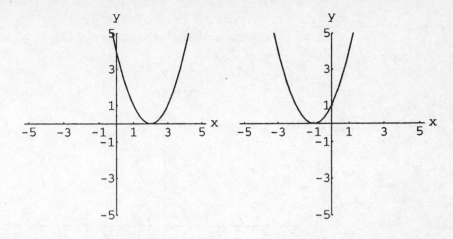

$$f(x) = (x-2)^2 \qquad\qquad f(x) = (x+1)^2$$

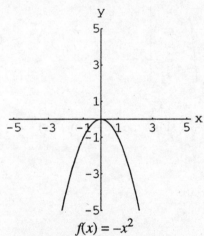

$$f(x) = -x^2$$

Note that several transformations can be combined to shift a graph up or down *and* to the right or left. Study the following example.

EXAMPLE 4

Describe each transformation and then sketch the function.

a) $f(x) = x^3 + 1$

b) $f(x) = \sqrt{x} - 3$

c) $f(x) = |x - 3|$

d) $f(x) = |x + 1| - 4$

e) $f(x) = -x^2 + 2$

SOLUTION 4

a) $f(x) = x^3 + 1$ shifts the graph of $f(x) = x^3$ upward 1 unit.

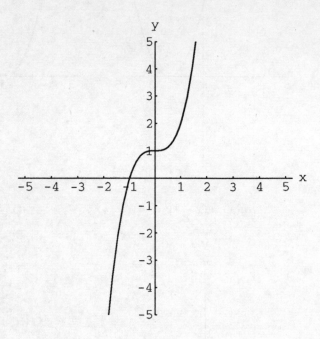

b) $f(x) = \sqrt{x} - 3$ shifts the graph of $f(x) = \sqrt{x}$ downward 3 units.

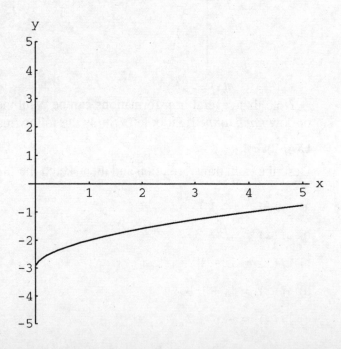

c) $f(x) = |x - 3|$ shifts the graph of $f(x) = |x|$ to the right 3 units.

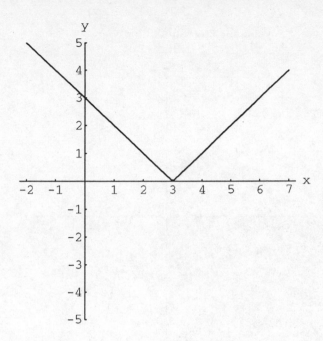

d) $f(x) = |x + 1| - 4$ shifts the graph of $f(x) = |x|$ to the left 1 unit and downward 4 units.

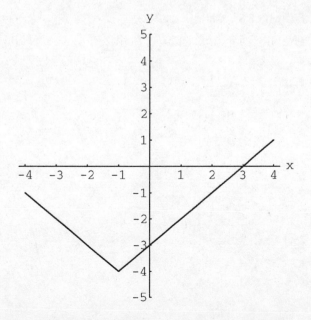

e) $f(x) = -x^2 + 2$ shifts the graph of $f(x) = x^2$ upward 2 units and reflects the graph about the *x*-axis.

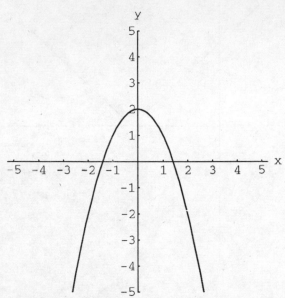

Note in examples with combinations of transformations (like d and e) that you may change the order in which you transform the graph and still arrive at the correct solution.

EXAMPLE 5

Use the graph of $f(x) = x^2$ to determine a formula for the given function.

a)   b)

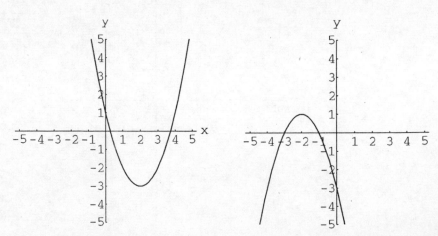

SOLUTION 5

a) Since the curve has been shifted to the right 2 units and down 3 units, the equation of the graph is $f(x) = (x-2)^2 - 3$.

b) Since the curve has been shifted to the left 2 units, up 1 unit, and reflected about the *x*-axis, the equation of the graph is
$$f(x) = -(x+2)^2 + 1$$

Operations with Functions

Just as we can add, subtract, multiply and divide numbers, we can add, subtract, multiply and divide functions.

Definitions.

If *f* and *g* are functions,

$(f + g)(x) = f(x) + g(x)$

$(f - g)(x) = f(x) - g(x)$

$(fg)(x) = f(x)g(x)$

$$\frac{f}{g}(x) = \frac{f(x)}{g(x)}, g(x) \neq 0$$

EXAMPLE 6

If $f(x) = 2x + 5$ and $g(x) = x^2 - 2x + 1$, find

a) $(f + g)(3)$

b) $(fg)(-1)$

c) $\dfrac{f}{g}(0)$

SOLUTION 6

a) $(f + g)(3)$

$= f(3) + g(3)$ Use $(f + g)(x) = f(x) + g(x)$.

$= 2(3) + 5 + (3)^2 - 2(3) + 1$ Substitute $x = 3$.

$= 6 + 5 + 9 - 6 + 1$ Simplify.

$= 15$

b) $(fg)(-1)$

$= f(-1)g(-1)$ Use $(fg)(x) = f(x)g(x)$.

$= [2(-1) + 5][(-1)^2 - 2(-1) + 1]$ Substitute $x = -1$.

$= (3)(4)$ Simplify inside each set of

brackets.

$= 12$

c) $\dfrac{f}{g}(0)$

$= \dfrac{f(0)}{g(0)}$ Use $\dfrac{f}{g}(x) = \dfrac{f(x)}{g(x)}$

$= \dfrac{2(0)+5}{(0)^2 - 2(0) + 1}$ Substitute $x = 0$.

$= \dfrac{5}{1} = 5$ Simplify.

EXAMPLE 7

If $f(x) = 3x^2 - 5x - 4$ and $g(x) = 2x + 3$, find

a) $(f - g)(x)$

b) $(fg)(x)$

c) $\dfrac{f}{g}(x)$

SOLUTION 7

a) $(f - g)(x)$

$= f(x) - g(x)$ Use the definition of function subtraction.

$= (3x^2 - 5x - 4) - (2x + 3)$ Substitute.

$= 3x^2 - 5x - 4 - 2x - 3$ Subtract.

$= 3x^2 - 7x - 7$ Combine similar terms.

b) $(fg)(x)$

$= f(x)g(x)$ Use the definition of function multiplication.

$= (3x^2 - 5x - 4)(2x + 3)$ Substitute.

$= 6x^3 + 9x^2 - 10x^2 - 15x - 8x - 12$ Distribute.

$= 6x^3 - x^2 - 23x - 12$ Combine similar terms.

c) $\dfrac{f}{g}(x)$

$$= \frac{f(x)}{g(x)}$$

Use the definition of
function division.

$$= \frac{3x^2 - 5x - 4}{2x + 3}$$

Substitute.

Composition of Functions

In addition to the four basic operations (addition, subtraction, multiplication, division), we can also compose functions.

Definition.

The composition of functions f and g, written $f \circ g$ is
$f \circ g = f(g(x))$

The composition of functions indicates an order of evaluating the functions. $(f \circ g)(3) = f(g(3))$ means first evaluate $g(3)$, then evaluate f at the resulting value.

EXAMPLE 8

If $f(x) = 3x + 1$ and $g(x) = -2x - 4$, find $(f \circ g)(3)$.
SOLUTION 8
$(f \circ g)(3)$

$\quad = f(g(3))$ Use the definition of
composition of functions.

$\quad = f(-2(3) - 4)$ Find $g(3)$.

$\quad = f(-10)$ Now evaluate $f(-10)$.

$\quad = 3(-10) + 1$ Substitute $x = -10$.

$\quad = -29$

EXAMPLE 9

If $f(x) = 3x + 1$ and $g(x) = -2x - 4$, find $(g \circ f)(3)$.
SOLUTION 9
$(g \circ f)(3)$

$\quad = g(f(3))$

$\quad = g(3(3) + 1)$ Find $f(3)$.

$\quad = g(10)$ Now evaluate $g(10)$.

$\quad = -2(10) - 4$ Substitute $x = 10$.

$\quad = -24$

Notice from examples 8 and 9 that in general $g \circ f \neq f \circ g$.

EXAMPLE 10

If $f(x) = x^2 - 1$ and $g(x) = 3x + 4$, find $f \circ g$ and $g \circ f$.

SOLUTION 10

$f \circ g$ means $(f \circ g)(x) = f(g(x))$.

We know $g(x) = 3x + 4$, so we must find $f(3x + 4)$.

$f(3x + 4)$

$\quad = (3x + 4)^2 - 1$ Replace x with $3x + 4$.

$\quad = 9x^2 + 24x + 16 - 1$ Multiply.

$\quad = 9x^2 + 24x + 15$ Add similar terms.

$g \circ f = (g \circ f)(x) = g(f(x))$

We know $f(x) = x^2 - 1$, so we must find $g(x^2 - 1)$.

$g(x^2 - 1) =$

$\quad = 3(x^2 - 1) + 4$ Replace x with $x^2 - 1$.

$\quad = 3x^2 - 3 + 4$ Multiply.

$\quad = 3x^2 + 1$ Add similar terms.

2.2 REVIEW OF THE TRIGONOMETRIC FUNCTIONS

The trigonometry topics in this section are presented as a review. The formulas and definitions are those which we will use in the remainder of the text. The trigonometric functions are usually defined using either a right triangle or a point on the terminal side of an angle. Both definitions are presented.

Definitions of the Trigonometric Functions

Given a right triangle with side lengths labeled as shown,

$$\sin\theta = \frac{\text{opposite}}{\text{hypotenuse}} \qquad \csc\theta = \frac{\text{hypotenuse}}{\text{opposite}}$$

$$\cos\theta = \frac{\text{adjacent}}{\text{hypotenuse}} \qquad \sec\theta = \frac{\text{hypotenuse}}{\text{adjacent}}$$

$$\tan\theta = \frac{\text{opposite}}{\text{adjacent}} \qquad \cot\theta = \frac{\text{adjacent}}{\text{hypotenuse}}$$

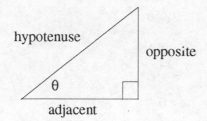

Given a point (x, y) on the terminal side of an angle θ where

$$r = \sqrt{x^2 + y^2},$$

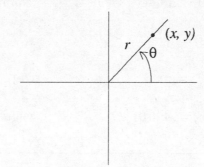

$$\sin\theta = \frac{y}{r} \qquad\qquad \csc\theta = \frac{r}{y}$$

$$\cos\theta = \frac{x}{r} \qquad\qquad \sec\theta = \frac{r}{x}$$

$$\tan\theta = \frac{y}{x} \qquad\qquad \cot\theta = \frac{x}{y}$$

The fundamental identities can be derived from these definitions.

Fundamental Identities

Reciprocal Identities

$$\sin\theta = \frac{1}{\csc\theta} \qquad\qquad \csc\theta = \frac{1}{\sin\theta}$$

$$\cos\theta = \frac{1}{\sec\theta} \qquad\qquad \sec\theta = \frac{1}{\cos\theta}$$

$$\tan\theta = \frac{1}{\cot\theta} = \frac{\sin\theta}{\cos\theta} \qquad\qquad \cot\theta = \frac{1}{\tan\theta} = \frac{\cos\theta}{\sin\theta}$$

Pythagorean Identities
$$\sin^2\theta + \cos^2\theta = 1$$

$$1 + \tan^2\theta = \sec^2\theta$$

$$1 + \cot^2\theta = \csc^2\theta$$

The following identities will also be useful in this course.

Negative angles:

$$\sin(-\theta) = -\sin\theta$$

$$\cos(-\theta) = \cos\theta$$

$$\tan(-\theta) = -\tan\theta$$

Sum or Difference of two angles:

$$\sin(a \pm b) = \sin a\cos b \pm \cos a\sin b$$

$$\cos(a \pm b) = \cos a\cos b \mp \sin a\sin b$$

$$\tan(a \pm b) = \frac{\tan a \pm \tan b}{1 \pm \tan a\tan b}$$

Double-angle formulas:

$$\sin 2\theta = 2\sin\theta\cos\theta$$

$$\cos 2\theta = 2\cos^2\theta - 1 = 1 - 2\sin^2\theta = \cos^2\theta - \sin^2\theta$$

Half-angle formulas:

$$\sin\frac{\theta}{2} = \pm\sqrt{\frac{1 - \cos\theta}{2}}$$

$$\cos\frac{\theta}{2} = \pm\sqrt{\frac{1 + \cos\theta}{2}}$$

$$\tan\frac{\theta}{2} = \pm\sqrt{\frac{1 - \cos\theta}{1 + \cos\theta}}$$

Special Angles

You should also memorize the trigonometric function values of the special angles, $\pi/6$ or $30°$, $\pi/4$ or $45°$, and $\pi/3$ or $60°$.

	$\frac{\pi}{6}$ or $30°$	$\frac{\pi}{4}$ or $45°$	$\frac{\pi}{3}$ or $60°$
sin	$\frac{1}{2}$	$\frac{\sqrt{2}}{2}$	$\frac{\sqrt{3}}{2}$
cos	$\frac{\sqrt{3}}{2}$	$\frac{\sqrt{2}}{2}$	$\frac{1}{2}$
tan	$\frac{\sqrt{3}}{3}$	1	$\sqrt{3}$

Two quick sketches will help you remember the values of the trigonometric functions at these special angles.

For $30°$ and $60°$, draw an equilateral triangle measuring 2 units on each side. Draw in the altitude to form a $30°$, $60°$, $90°$ triangle as shown:

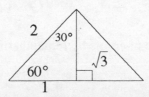

For 45°, draw a square measuring 1 unit on each side. Draw in a diagonal to form a 45°, 45°, 90° triangle as shown:

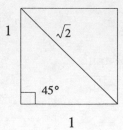

The hypotenuse (side opposite the right angle) has been found in each case by using the Pythagorean theorem. $(c^2 = a^2 + b^2)$.

Reference Angles

We can find the values of the trigonometric functions for angles in quadrants other than quadrant I using reference angles and a sign chart. The **reference angle** for an angle θ is the positive acute angle measured from the terminal side of θ to the x-axis. Study the following chart.

For $0 < \theta < 2\pi$, locate the terminal side of θ in a quadrant. Then the reference angle θ_{ref} equals:

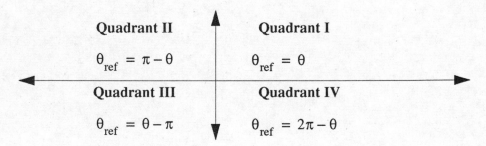

To find the appropriate sign of each function, use the following chart. The indicated functions and their reciprocals are positive, and the other functions are negative.

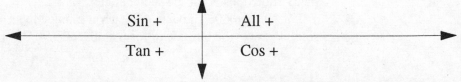

Many students remember this by remembering "<u>A</u>ll <u>S</u>tudents <u>T</u>ake <u>C</u>alculus."

Radians and Degrees

Finally, angles are measured using radians in calculus (this makes the trigonometric functions have domains of real numbers). To convert from radians to degrees or degrees to radians use:

Conversion Factors

To convert degrees to radians, multiply by $\dfrac{\pi}{180°}$.

To convert radians to degrees, multiply by $\dfrac{180°}{\pi}$.

When calculators are used, remember that the calculator must be in the appropriate **mode**, either radian or degree. If no degree symbol is shown, radian mode is implied. Thus, sin 2 means the sine of 2 radians.

EXAMPLE 11

Express each angle in radian measure as a multiple of π.

a) 210°

b) 315°

SOLUTION 11

a) $210° = 210° \cdot \dfrac{\pi}{180°}$ 　　　　　　Multiply by $\dfrac{\pi}{180°}$.

$= \dfrac{7}{6}\pi$ or $\dfrac{7\pi}{6}$ 　　　　　　Reduce $\dfrac{210}{180} = \dfrac{7}{6}$.

b) $315° = 315° \cdot \dfrac{\pi}{180°}$ 　　　　　　Multiply by $\dfrac{\pi}{180°}$.

$= \dfrac{7}{4}\pi$ or $\dfrac{7\pi}{4}$ 　　　　　　Reduce $\dfrac{315}{180} = \dfrac{7}{4}$.

EXAMPLE 12

Express each angle in degrees.

a) $\dfrac{3}{2}\pi$

b) $-\dfrac{2}{3}\pi$

SOLUTION 12

a) $\dfrac{3}{2}\pi = \dfrac{3\pi}{2} \cdot \dfrac{180°}{\pi}$ 　　　　　　Multiply by $\dfrac{180°}{\pi}$.

$$= 270°$$ $$\frac{3}{2} \cdot 180 = 270°.$$

b) $-\dfrac{2}{3}\pi = -\dfrac{2\pi}{3} \cdot \dfrac{180°}{\pi}$ Multiply by $\dfrac{180°}{\pi}$.

$$= -120°$$ $$-\dfrac{2}{3} \cdot 180 = -120°.$$

EXAMPLE 13

Solve each equation for $\theta, 0 \le \theta < 2\pi$.
a) $4\sin^2\theta - 1 = 0$

b) $\tan\theta\cos\theta = \cos\theta$

c) $\sin^2\theta + \cos\theta - 1 = 0$

SOLUTION 13

a) $4\sin^2\theta - 1 = 0$ This is a quadratic equation.

$(2\sin\theta - 1)(2\sin\theta + 1) = 0$ Factor.

$2\sin\theta - 1 = 0$ or $2\sin\theta + 1 = 0$ Set each factor equal to 0.

$\sin\theta = \dfrac{1}{2}$ or $\sin\theta = -\dfrac{1}{2}$ Solve each equation.

Referring to the special angles, the reference angle is $\dfrac{\pi}{6}$ (or 30°) since $\sin\dfrac{\pi}{6} = \dfrac{1}{2}$. $\sin\theta = \dfrac{1}{2}$ if θ is in quadrant I or II.

In quadrant II: $\pi - \dfrac{\pi}{6} = \dfrac{6\pi}{6} - \dfrac{1\pi}{6} = \dfrac{5\pi}{6}$.

$\sin\theta = -\dfrac{1}{2}$ if θ is in quadrant III or IV.

In quadrant III: $\pi + \dfrac{\pi}{6} = \dfrac{6\pi}{6} + \dfrac{1\pi}{6} = \dfrac{7\pi}{6}$.

In quadrant IV: $2\pi - \dfrac{\pi}{6} = \dfrac{12\pi}{6} - \dfrac{1\pi}{6} = \dfrac{11\pi}{6}$

So $\theta = \dfrac{\pi}{6}, \dfrac{5\pi}{6}, \dfrac{7\pi}{6}$ or $\dfrac{11\pi}{6}$.

b) $\tan\theta\cos\theta = \cos\theta$

$\tan\theta\cos\theta - \cos\theta = 0$ Get 0 on one side.

$\cos\theta(\tan\theta - 1) = 0$ Factor.

$\cos\theta = 0$ or $\tan\theta - 1 = 0$ Set each factor equal to 0.

$\cos\theta = 0$ or $\tan\theta = 1$ Solve each equation.

$\cos\theta = 0$ when $\theta = \dfrac{\pi}{2}$ or $\dfrac{3\pi}{2}$.

$\tan\theta = 1$ means the reference angle is $\dfrac{\pi}{4}$ since $\tan\dfrac{\pi}{4} = 1$.
The tangent is positive in quadrants I and III.

In quadrant III, $\pi + \dfrac{\pi}{4} = \dfrac{4\pi}{4} + \dfrac{1\pi}{4} = \dfrac{5\pi}{4}$.

So $\theta = \dfrac{\pi}{2}, \dfrac{3\pi}{2}, \dfrac{\pi}{4}$ or $\dfrac{5\pi}{4}$.

c) $\sin^2\theta + \cos\theta - 1 = 0$

$1 - \cos^2\theta + \cos\theta - 1 = 0$ Use the Pythagorean
                                          identity $\sin^2\theta = 1 - \cos^2\theta$
                                          to replace $\sin^2\theta$.

$-\cos^2\theta + \cos\theta = 0$ Add similar terms.

$-\cos\theta(\cos\theta - 1) = 0$ Factor.

$-\cos\theta = 0$ or $\cos\theta - 1 = 0$ Set each factor equal to 0.

$\cos\theta = 0$ or $\cos\theta = 1$ Solve each equation.

$\theta = \dfrac{\pi}{2}$ or $\dfrac{3\pi}{2}$ or $\theta = 0$

So $\theta = \dfrac{\pi}{2}, \dfrac{3\pi}{2}$ or 0.

2.3 LIMITS AND LIMIT PROOFS

When we look at a graph of $f(x) = x^2$, we observe that the point $(2, 4)$ is on the graph. If we remove this point, leaving a small hole in the graph, we can use the concept of a limit to describe the fact that the y value gets close to 4 as the x value gets close to 2. Using limits, we say

$$\lim_{x \to 2} x^2 = 4$$

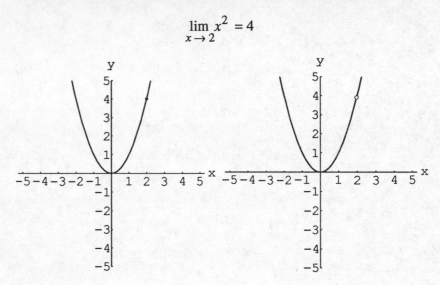

$\varepsilon - \delta$ *Definition of a Limit*

The ε-δ (epsilon-delta) definition of a limit can be used to prove that a y-value approaches some number L when the x-value approaches some number c.

Definition of a Limit

The statement $\lim_{x \to c} f(x) = L$ means that for each $\varepsilon > 0$ there

exists a $\delta > 0$ such that if $0 < |x - c| < \delta$ then $|f(x) - L| < \varepsilon$.

Since this definition is in the if-then form, we must start with the "if" statement and end at the "then" statement. However, it's often easier to work on scratch paper with $|f(x) - L| < \varepsilon$ and find the necessary relationship between ε and δ.

EXAMPLE 14

Use the ε-δ definition to prove $\lim\limits_{x \to 4} (3x - 2) = 10$.

SOLUTION 14

We begin by writing the ε-δ definition with $f(x) = 3x - 2$, $c = 4$ and $L = 10$:

If $0 < |x - 4| < \delta$ then $|(3x - 2) - 10| < \varepsilon$.

On scratch paper:

$|(3x - 2) - 10| < \varepsilon$	Work on $|f(x) - L| < \varepsilon$.
$|3x - 12| < \varepsilon$	Simplify.
$|3(x - 4)| < \varepsilon$	Factor.
$|3||x - 4| < \varepsilon$	Use $|ab| = |a| \cdot |b|$.
$|x - 4| < \dfrac{\varepsilon}{3}$	$|3| = 3$. Divide both sides by 3.

The proof:

Let $\delta = \dfrac{\varepsilon}{3}$.

$|x - 4| < \delta$	Begin with the "if" statement.
$|x - 4| < \dfrac{\varepsilon}{3}$	Replace δ with $\dfrac{\varepsilon}{3}$.
$3|x - 4| < \varepsilon$	Multiply both sides by 3.
$|3||x - 4| < \varepsilon$	$3 = |3|$.
$|3(x - 4)| < \varepsilon$	Use $|a| \cdot |b| = |a \cdot b|$.
$|3x - 12| < \varepsilon$	Use the distributive property.
$|(3x - 2) - 10| < \varepsilon$	Write -12 as $-2 - 10$.

EXAMPLE 15

Use the ε-δ to prove that $\lim\limits_{x \to 2} (x^2 - 3x + 1) = -1$.

SOLUTION 15

Write the ε-δ definition with $f(x) = x^2 - 3x + 1$, $c = 2$, and $L = -1$:

If $0 < |x - 2| < \delta$ then $\left| (x^2 - 3x + 1) - (-1) \right| < \varepsilon$.

On scratch paper:

$\left\| (x^2 - 3x + 1) - (-1) \right\| < \varepsilon$	Work on $\|f(x) - L\| < \varepsilon$.
$\left\|x^2 - 3x + 2\right\| < \varepsilon$	Simplify.
$\| (x - 2)(x - 1) \| < \varepsilon$	Factor.
$\|x - 2\|\|x - 1\| < \varepsilon$	Use $\|a \cdot b\| = \|a\| \cdot \|b\|$.

We know we can make $|x - 2|$ as small as we wish, for example let $\delta \le 1$.

Then

$\|x - 2\| < 1$	$\|x - 2\| < \delta$.
$-1 < x - 2 < 1$	Use $\|x\| < a \Leftrightarrow -a < x < a$.
$1 < x < 3$	Add 2.
$1 - 1 < x - 1 < 3 - 1$	Subtract 1.
$0 < x - 1 < 2$	Simplify.
$\|x - 1\| < 2$	

Since $|x - 2| < \delta$ and $|x - 1| < 2$, if we require $\delta < \dfrac{\varepsilon}{2}$, then $|x - 2||x - 1| < \varepsilon$.

The proof:

Let δ be the minimum of $\dfrac{\varepsilon}{2}$ and 1.

$\|x - 2\| < \delta$	Begin with the "if" statement.

$$|x-2||x-1| < \delta|x-1| \qquad\qquad \text{Multiply by } |x-1|.$$

$$|(x-2)(x-1)| < \delta|x-1| \qquad\qquad \text{Use } |a||b| = |ab|.$$

$$\left|x^2 - 3x + 2\right| < \delta|x-1| < \frac{\varepsilon}{2}(2) \qquad\qquad \text{Use } \delta = \frac{\varepsilon}{2} \text{ and the fact}$$
$$\text{that } |x-1| < 2.$$

$$\left|x^2 - 3x + 2\right| < \varepsilon$$

$$\left|(x^2 - 3x + 1) - (-1)\right| < \varepsilon \qquad\qquad \text{Write } 2 = 1 - (-1).$$

2.4 EVALUATING LIMITS

Using the ε-δ definition to prove that a limit exists can be tedious (to say the least). Fortunately, there are many theorems that allow us to simplify the process of evaluating a limit. These theorems can be found in any standard text. They can be summarized by the following guidelines.

To Evaluate $\lim\limits_{x \to c} f(x)$

1. Substitute c for x in $f(x)$.
2. If the resulting answer exists, that answer is the limit.
3. If the substitution results in a division by 0, use algebraic tecniques to produce an equivalent function which can be evaluated by substitution.

EXAMPLE 16

Find each limit.

a) $\lim\limits_{x \to 3} 2x^2 + 1$

b) $\lim\limits_{x \to -1} \dfrac{x-2}{x+3}$

c) $\lim\limits_{x \to \frac{\pi}{2}} \sin 2x$

SOLUTION 16

a) $\lim\limits_{x \to 3} 2x^2 + 1 = 2(3)^2 + 1$ Substitute 3 for x.

$= 2(9) + 1$ Simplify exponents.

$= 19$ Multiply and then add.

b) $\lim\limits_{x \to -1} \dfrac{x-2}{x+3} = \dfrac{(-1)-2}{(-1)+3}$ Substitute -1 for x.

$= -\dfrac{3}{2}$ Simplify.

c) $\lim\limits_{x \to \frac{\pi}{2}} \sin 2x = \sin 2\left(\dfrac{\pi}{2}\right)$ Substitute $\dfrac{\pi}{2}$ for x.

$= \sin \pi$ Simplify.

$= 0$

EXAMPLE 17

Find each limit.

a) $\lim\limits_{x \to 2} \dfrac{x^2-4}{x-2}$

b) $\lim\limits_{x \to 0} \dfrac{\sqrt{x+9}-3}{x}$

SOLUTION 17

a) $\lim\limits_{x \to 2} \dfrac{x^2-4}{x-2} = \dfrac{(2)^2-4}{(2)-2}$ Substitute 2 for x.

$= \dfrac{0}{0}$ Division by 0 is not defined.

Substitution resulted in division by 0. Use algebraic techniques.

$\lim\limits_{x \to 2} \dfrac{x^2-4}{x-2} = \lim\limits_{x \to 2} \dfrac{(x-2)(x+2)}{x-2}$ Factor.

$= \lim\limits_{x \to 2} x + 2$ $\dfrac{x-2}{x-2} = 1$

$$= (2) + 2 \qquad \text{Substitute 2 for } x.$$
$$= 4$$

b) $\lim\limits_{x \to 0} \dfrac{\sqrt{x+9} - 3}{x}$

Substituting 0 for x will result in division by 0. Use algebraic techniques.

$$\lim_{x \to 0} \frac{\sqrt{x+9}-3}{x} \cdot \frac{\sqrt{x+9}+3}{\sqrt{x+9}+3} \qquad \begin{array}{l}\text{Multiply by the conjugate} \\ \text{of the numerator.}\end{array}$$

$$= \lim_{x \to 0} \frac{x+9-9}{x(\sqrt{x+9}+3)} \qquad \text{Multiply the numerators.}$$

$$= \lim_{x \to 0} \frac{x+9-9}{x(\sqrt{x+9}+3)} \qquad \text{Simplify the numerator.}$$

$$= \frac{1}{\sqrt{(0)+9}+3} \qquad \text{Substitute 0 for } x.$$

$$= \frac{1}{\sqrt{9}+3} = \frac{1}{6} \qquad \text{Simplify the denominator.}$$

Trigonometric Limits

Some trigonometric functions can be evaluated by direct substitution (see Example 16c). Others may require the use of the fundamental trigonometric identities (see section 2.2) or the use of the following special limits.

$$\lim_{x \to 0} \frac{\sin x}{x} = 1 \qquad\qquad \lim_{x \to 0} \frac{1 - \cos x}{x} = 0$$

EXAMPLE 18

Find each limit.

a) $\lim\limits_{x \to \pi} \dfrac{\sin x}{\cos x}$

b) $\lim\limits_{x \to \frac{\pi}{2}} \dfrac{\cot x}{\cos x}$

c) $\lim\limits_{x \to 0} \dfrac{\sin 5x}{x}$

d) $\lim\limits_{x \to 0} \dfrac{1 - \cos^2 x}{x}$

SOLUTION 18

a) $\lim\limits_{x \to \pi} \dfrac{\sin x}{\cos x} = \dfrac{\sin(\pi)}{\cos(\pi)}$ | Substitute π for x.

$= \dfrac{0}{-1}$ | Evaluate.

$= 0$ | Simplify.

b) $\lim\limits_{x \to \frac{\pi}{2}} \dfrac{\cot x}{\cos x} = \dfrac{\cot\left(\frac{\pi}{2}\right)}{\cos\left(\frac{\pi}{2}\right)}$ | Substitute $\dfrac{\pi}{2}$ for x.

$= \dfrac{0}{0}$ | Division by 0 is not defined.

Substitution resulted in division by 0. Use the fundamental trigonometric identities.

$\lim\limits_{x \to \frac{\pi}{2}} \dfrac{\cot x}{\cos x} = \lim\limits_{x \to \frac{\pi}{2}} \dfrac{\frac{\cos x}{\sin x}}{\frac{\cos x}{1}}$ | Write $\cot x = \dfrac{\cos x}{\sin x}$.

$= \lim\limits_{x \to \frac{\pi}{2}} \dfrac{\cos x}{\sin x} \cdot \dfrac{1}{\cos x}$ | Invert and multiply.

$= \lim\limits_{x \to \frac{\pi}{2}} \dfrac{1}{\sin x}$ | $\dfrac{\cos x}{\cos x} = 1$.

$= \dfrac{1}{\sin\left(\frac{\pi}{2}\right)}$ | Substitute $\dfrac{\pi}{2}$ for x.

$$= \frac{1}{1} = 1$$

Simplify.

c) $\lim\limits_{x \to 0} \dfrac{\sin 5x}{x}$

Substituting 0 for x will result in division by 0. We'll use $\lim\limits_{x \to 0} \dfrac{\sin x}{x}$.

$$= \lim\limits_{x \to 0} \frac{5}{5} \cdot \frac{\sin 5x}{x}$$

Multiply by a form of 1.

$$= \lim\limits_{x \to 0} \frac{5 \sin 5x}{5x}$$

Multiply the numerators and denominators.

$$= 5 \lim\limits_{x \to 0} \frac{\sin 5x}{5x}$$

Factor out the 5.

$$= 5(1)$$

$\lim\limits_{x \to 0} \dfrac{\sin 5x}{5x} = 1$

$$= 5$$

Note that $x \to 0$, $5x \to 0$ so the limit theorem applies.

d) $\lim\limits_{x \to 0} \dfrac{1 - \cos^2 x}{x}$

Substituting 0 for x will result in division by 0. We'll use

$\lim\limits_{x \to 0} \dfrac{1 - \cos^2 x}{x} = 0$.

$$= \lim\limits_{x \to 0} \frac{(1 - \cos x)(1 + \cos x)}{x}$$

Factor.

$$= \lim\limits_{x \to 0} (\frac{1 - \cos x}{x})(1 + \cos x)$$

$$= \quad 0(1 + \cos 0)$$

Use $\lim\limits_{x \to 0} \dfrac{1 - \cos x}{x} = 0$.

$$= 0(2)$$

$$= 0$$

Substitute 0 for x.

Simplify.

2.5 ONE-SIDED LIMITS AND CONTINUITY

A graphing interpretation of $\lim_{x \to c} f(x) = L$ means that the function

$f(x)$ approaches a y-value of L as x approaches c from both the left side and right side. If we wish to restrict our view to one side of x, we use the following.

Notation	Meaning
$\lim_{x \to c^+} f(x) = M$	As x approaches c *from the right*, $f(x)$ approaches M.
$\lim_{x \to c^-} f(x) = N$	As x approaches c *from the left*, $f(x)$ approaches N.

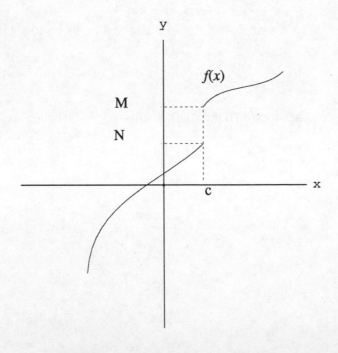

EXAMPLE 19

Find each limit for the function *f*.

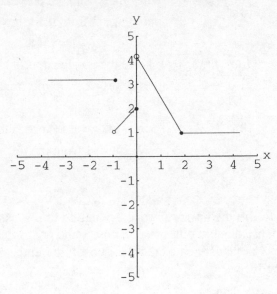

a) $\lim\limits_{x \to 0^+} f(x)$

b) $\lim\limits_{x \to 0^-} f(x)$

c) $\lim\limits_{x \to 2^-} f(x)$

d) $\lim\limits_{x \to -1^+} f(x)$

e) $\lim\limits_{x \to -1^-} f(x)$

SOLUTION 19

a) $\lim\limits_{x \to 0^+} f(x) = 4$ since the *y*-value approaches 4 as the *x*-value
approaches 0 from the right.

b) $\lim\limits_{x \to 0^-} f(x) = 2$ since the *y*-value approaches 2 as the *x*-value approaches 0 from the left.

c) $\lim\limits_{x \to 2^-} f(x) = 1$ since the *y*-value approaches 1 as the *x*-value
approaches 2 from the left.

d) $\lim\limits_{x \to -1^+} f(x) = 1$ since the *y*-value approaches 1 as the *x*-value
approaches –1 from the right.

e) $\lim\limits_{x \to -1^-} f(x) = 3$ since the *y*-value approaches 3 as the *x*-value
approaches –1 from the left.

Evaluating
One-sided Limits
Given an Equation
Recall the basic rules for evaluating limits - substitute whenever possible, use algebra otherwise. Those same principles apply to one-sided limits. Care must be taken not to substitute mindlessly. Study Example 20e) carefully.

EXAMPLE 20

Find each limit.

a) $\lim\limits_{x \to 1^-} x^2 - 4x + 1$

b) $\lim\limits_{x \to 3^+} \dfrac{x^2 - 9}{x - 3}$

c) $\lim\limits_{x \to 2^+} \dfrac{|x - 2|}{x - 2}$

d) $\lim\limits_{x \to 2^-} \dfrac{|x - 2|}{x - 2}$

e) $\lim\limits_{x \to 4^-} \sqrt{x - 4}$

SOLUTION 20

a) $\lim\limits_{x \to 1^-} x^2 - 4x + 1$

$= (1)^2 - 4(1) + 1$ Substitute 1 for x.

$= 6$ Simplify.

b) $\lim\limits_{x \to 3^+} \dfrac{x^2 - 9}{x - 3}$

Substituting 3 for x results in division by 0. Use algebra to factor and reduce:

$\lim\limits_{x \to 3^+} \dfrac{x^2 - 9}{x - 3} = \lim\limits_{x \to 3^+} \dfrac{(x-3)(x+3)}{x-3}$ Factor.

$= \lim\limits_{x \to 3^+} x + 3$ $\dfrac{x-3}{x-3} = 1$.

$= 3 + 3$ Substitute 3 for x.

$= 6$ Simplify.

c) $\lim\limits_{x \to 2^+} \dfrac{|x - 2|}{x - 2}$

Substituting 2 for x results in division by 0. Since the numerator does not factor, we reason as follows. As x approaches 2 from the right, $x - 2 > 0$. This implies that $|x - 2| = x - 2$ since the number in the absolute value bars is positive. Then,

$\lim\limits_{x \to 2^+} \dfrac{|x - 2|}{x - 2} = \lim\limits_{x \to 2^+} \dfrac{x - 2}{x - 2} = \lim\limits_{x \to 2^+} 1 = 1$

d) $\lim\limits_{x \to 2^-} \dfrac{|x - 2|}{x - 2}$

As x approaches 2 from the left, $x - 2 < 0$. This implies that $|x - 2| = -(x - 2)$. Then

$\lim\limits_{x \to 2^-} \dfrac{|x - 2|}{x - 2} = \lim\limits_{x \to 2^-} \dfrac{-(x - 2)}{x - 2} = -1$

e) $\lim\limits_{x \to 4^-} \sqrt{x - 4}$

Substituting 4 for x would lead to the *incorrect* answer 0. Consider

the graph of $f(x) = \sqrt{x-4}$:

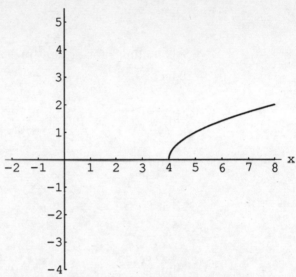

There is no graph as x approaches 4 from the left. Therefore,

$\lim\limits_{x \to 4^-} \sqrt{x-4}$ does not exist.

Note that $\lim\limits_{x \to c} f(x) = L$ means that both the limit from the left *and* the

limit from the right as x approaches c must exist and be equal.

EXAMPLE 21

Find $\lim\limits_{x \to 2} \dfrac{|x-2|}{x-2}$.

SOLUTION 21

We found in Example 20 that $\lim\limits_{x \to 2^+} \dfrac{|x-2|}{x-2} = 1$ and

$\lim\limits_{x \to 2^-} \dfrac{|x-2|}{x-2} = -1$.

Since these limits are not equal, $\lim\limits_{x \to 2} \dfrac{|x-2|}{x-2}$ does not exist.

Continuity

A function is continuous when the graph can be draw without breaks or holes. To link an algebraic meaning to this concept, we must meet three conditions for a function to be continuous at a point:

1. The function must exist at that point.
2. The limit at that point must exist.
3. The function value and the limit value at that point must be equal.

EXAMPLE 22

Determine whether the function is continuous at the given point.

a) $f(x) = x^2 + 3x - 1$ at $x = -1$

b) $f(x) = \dfrac{x^2 - 9}{x - 3}$ at $x = 3$

c) $f(x) = \begin{cases} x^2 - 1 & x \neq 1 \\ 3 & x = 1 \end{cases}$

SOLUTION 22

a) $f(-1) = (-1)^2 + 3(-1) - 1$ Find $f(-1)$.

     $= -3$

     $\lim\limits_{x \to -1} x^2 - 3x - 1 = -3$ Find $\lim\limits_{x \to -1} f(x)$.

Since $f(-1) = \lim\limits_{x \to -1} f(x)$, the function is continuous at $x = -1$.

b) $f(3) = \dfrac{(3)^2 - 9}{(3) - 3} = \dfrac{0}{0}$ Find $f(3)$.

The function does not exist at $x = 3$ and therefore is not continuous at $x = 3$.

c) $f(1) = 3$ Find $f(1)$.

     $\lim\limits_{x \to 1} x^2 - 1 = (1)^2 - 1 = 0$ Find $\lim\limits_{x \to 1} f(x)$.

Since $f(1) \neq \lim_{x \to 1} f(x)$, the function is not continuous at $x = 1$.

EXAMPLE 23

At what points, if any, are the functions discontinuous?

a) $f(x) = x^3 - 1$

b) $f(x) = \dfrac{x - 2}{x^2 - x - 12}$

c) $f(x) = \begin{cases} 2x & x < 0 \\ x^2 & x \geq 0 \end{cases}$

d) $f(x) = \begin{cases} 2x & x < 1 \\ 3x + 4 & x \geq 1 \end{cases}$

SOLUTION 23

a) The function $f(x) = x^3 - 1$ has a domain of all real numbers.
    Thus, the function exists at all points. The limit at every point can be
    found by direct substitution without any resulting division by 0.
     Hence, the function has no discontinuities.

b) $f(x) = \dfrac{x - 2}{x^2 - x - 12} = \dfrac{x - 2}{(x - 4)(x + 3)}$ has a domain of all real .

numbers *except* 4 and −3. Since the function does not exist at these
points, it has discontinuities at $x = 4$ and $x = -3$.

c) The two pieces of this function are continuous on their domains.
    To determine if the pieces form a continuous function, consider the
    graph:

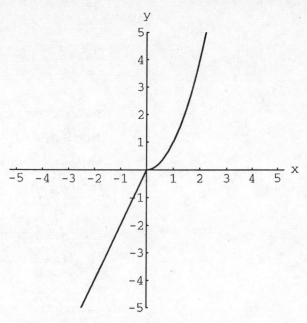

Check the *x*-value where the pieces are joined.

At $x = 0$,

$$f(0) = 0^2 = 0$$

$$\lim_{x \to 0^+} f(x) = 0^2 = 0 \qquad\qquad \lim_{x \to 0^-} f(x) = 2(0) = 0$$

Since $f(0) = \lim_{x \to 0} f(x)$, the function is continuous at 0.

d) Since $f(x) = 2x$ is continuous everywhere and $f(x) = 3x + 4$ is continuous everywhere, we only need to check $x = 1$.

$f(1) = 3(1) + 4 = 7$

$$\lim_{x \to 1^+} f(x) = 3(1) + 4 = 7 \qquad\qquad \lim_{x \to 1^-} f(x) = 2(1) = 2$$

Since the right-hand and left-hand limits are *not* equal, $\lim_{x \to 1} f(x)$

does not exist. Thus, the function is discontinuous at $x = 1$.

Practice Exercises

1. Find the domain.

a) $y = x^2 + 4$

b) $y = \dfrac{x+1}{x^2 + 5x + 6}$

c) $y = \sqrt{2x + 1}$

2. If $f(x) = \dfrac{x-3}{x+4}$ find

a) $f(-2)$

b) $f(0)$

c) $f(x + h)$

3. Sketch each graph making use of transformations.

a) $f(x) = x^2 - 3$

b) $f(x) = |x| + 2$

c) $f(x) = -\sqrt{x - 2}$

d) $f(x) = -(x+1)^2 + 4$

4. If $f(x) = x^2 - 4x + 2$ and

$g(x) = 2x + 1$ find

a) $(f - g)(x)$

b) $(fg)(x)$

c) $(f \circ g)(x)$

d) $(g \circ f)(x)$

5. Convert each angle to radians.

a) $135°$

b) $330°$

6. Convert each angle to degrees.

a) $\dfrac{7\pi}{4}$

b) $\dfrac{2\pi}{3}$

7. Solve each equation for $0 \le \theta < 2\pi$.

a) $4\cos^2\theta - 1 = 0$

b) $\sin\theta\cos\theta = \sin\theta$

c) $\tan^2\theta - \sec\theta - 1 = 0$

8. Use the ε-δ function to prove

a) $\lim_{x \to 3} 4x - 2 = 10$

b) $\lim_{x \to -1} 6x - 1 = -7$

9. Evaluate each limit.

a) $\lim_{x \to 2} x^2 - 6x$

b) $\lim_{x \to 1} \sqrt{3x + 5}$

c) $\lim_{x \to \frac{\pi}{4}} \dfrac{\sin 2x}{\cos x}$

10. Find each limit.

a) $\lim_{x \to 3} \dfrac{x^3 - 27}{x - 3}$

b) $\lim_{x \to -1} \dfrac{x^2 + 7x + 6}{x + 1}$

c) $\displaystyle \lim_{x \to 0} \frac{\dfrac{1}{x+2} - \dfrac{1}{2}}{x}$

11. Find each limit.

a) $\displaystyle \lim_{x \to 0} \frac{\sin 3x}{x}$

b) $\displaystyle \lim_{x \to 0} \frac{\sin 2x}{5x}$

c) $\displaystyle \lim_{x \to 0} \frac{\sin x - \sin x \cos x}{x^2}$

12. Find each limit.

a) $\displaystyle \lim_{x \to 1^+} \frac{6x - 1}{x + 2}$

b) $\displaystyle \lim_{x \to 3^+} \frac{x^2 - 6x + 9}{x - 3}$

c) $\displaystyle \lim_{x \to 2^-} \sqrt{2 + x}$

13. At what points, if any, are the functions discontinuous?

a) $f(x) = |x + 1|$

b) $f(x) = \dfrac{3x}{x^2 + 2x - 8}$

c) $f(x) = \begin{cases} -x & x < 0 \\ 2x^2 & 0 \le x < 3 \\ 4 & x \ge 3 \end{cases}$

Answers

1. a) all real numbers

    b) all real numbers except –3 and –2

    c) $\{x|\ (x \geq -\frac{1}{2})\}$

2. a) $-\frac{5}{2}$

    b) $-\frac{3}{4}$

    c) $\dfrac{x+h-3}{x+h+4}$

3. a)

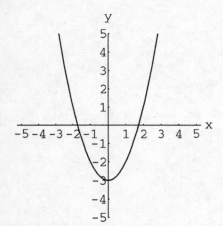

    b)

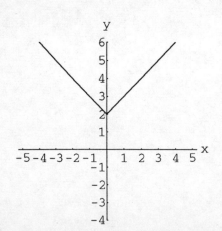

c)

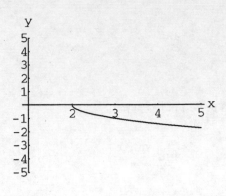

d)

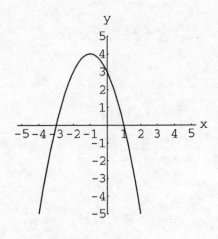

4. a) $x^2 - 6x + 1$

    b) $2x^3 - 7x^2 + 2$

    c) $4x^2 - 4x - 1$

    d) $2x^2 - 8x + 5$

5. a) $\dfrac{3\pi}{4}$

    b) $\dfrac{11\pi}{6}$

6. a) $315°$

    b) $120°$

7. a) $\dfrac{\pi}{3}, \dfrac{2\pi}{3}, \dfrac{4\pi}{3}, \dfrac{5\pi}{3}$

    b) $0, \pi$

    c) $\dfrac{\pi}{3}, \pi, \dfrac{5\pi}{3}$

8. a) If $0 < |x - 3| < \delta$ then

    $|(4x - 2) - 10| < \varepsilon$.

    Let $\delta = \dfrac{\varepsilon}{4}$.

    $|x - 3| < \delta \Rightarrow |x - 3| < \dfrac{\varepsilon}{4}$

    $\Rightarrow 4|x - 3| < \varepsilon$

    $\Rightarrow |4(x - 3)| < \varepsilon$

    $\Rightarrow |(4x - 2) - 10| < \varepsilon$

    b) If $0 < |x + 1| < \delta$ then

    $|(6x - 1) + 7| < \varepsilon$

    Let $\delta = \dfrac{\varepsilon}{6}$.

    $|x + 1| < \delta \Rightarrow |x + 1| < \dfrac{\varepsilon}{6}$

    $\Rightarrow 6|x + 1| < \varepsilon$

    $\Rightarrow |6(x + 1)| < \varepsilon$

    $\Rightarrow |(6x - 1) + 7| < \varepsilon$

9. a) -8

    b) $2\sqrt{2}$

    c) $\sqrt{2}$

10. a) 27

    b) 5

    c) $-\dfrac{1}{4}$

11. a) 3

    b) $\dfrac{2}{5}$

    c) 0

12. a) $\dfrac{5}{3}$

    b) 0

    c) does not exist

13. a) continuous everywhere

    b) discontinuous at $x = -4$ and $x = 2$

    c) discontinuous at $x = 3$

3

Derivatives

This chapter introduces one of the building blocks of calculus - derivatives. After a brief look at finding derivatives using the limit definition, we will use shortcuts to find derivatives of a variety of functions, including the trigonometric functions.

3.1 TANGENT LINES AND RATES OF CHANGE

Although we can easily find the slope of a line if we know either the equation of the line (by putting the equation in $y = mx + b$ form) or if we know two points on the line (using $m = \dfrac{y_2 - y_1}{x_2 - x_1}$), we cannot easily find the slope of a line that is tangent to a given curve. The slope of such a line, called a **tangent line**, can be found using

$$m = \lim_{\Delta x \to 0} \frac{f(x + \Delta x) - f(x)}{\Delta x}$$

where the line is tangent to the curve $y = f(x)$ at the point $(x, f(x))$.

To use this formula, follow these steps.

Finding the slope of the tangent
1. Find $f(x + \Delta x)$ by replacing x with $x + \Delta x$ in f.
2. Find $f(x)$.
3. Subtract and write the difference over Δx.
4. Find the limit, using algebra to help evaluate the limit when necessary.

Finding the Slope at a Specific Point

In the following example, we'll find the slope of the tangent at a specific point. Remember to replace x with the given x-coordinate. Do *not* replace Δx until we're ready to evaluate the limit.

EXAMPLE 1

Find the slope of the tangent to $f(x)$ at the given point.
a) $f(x) = 4x - 6$ at $(1, -2)$

b) $f(x) = x^2 - 3x$ at $(-1, 4)$

SOLUTION 1

a) $f(1 + \Delta x) = 4(1 + \Delta x) - 6$ Find $f(1 + \Delta x)$.

$\qquad\qquad\quad = 4 + 4\Delta x - 6$ Distribute.

$\qquad\qquad\quad = 4\Delta x - 2$ Add similar terms.

$f(1) = 4(1) - 6$ Find $f(1)$.

$\quad = -2$ Simplify.

$m = \lim\limits_{\Delta x \to 0} \dfrac{4\Delta x - 2 - (-2)}{\Delta x}$ Subtract and divide by Δx.

$\quad = \lim\limits_{\Delta x \to 0} \dfrac{4\Delta x - 2 + 2}{\Delta x}$ Find $\lim\limits_{\Delta x \to 0}$.

$\quad = \lim\limits_{\Delta x \to 0} \dfrac{4\Delta x}{\Delta x}$

$\quad = \lim\limits_{\Delta x \to 0} 4 = 0$

Thus the slope of the tangent to $f(x) = 4x - 6$ at the point $(1, -2)$ is 4.

b) $f(-1 + \Delta x) = (-1 + \Delta x)^2 - 3(-1 + \Delta x)$

Find $f(-1 + \Delta x)$.

$$= (1 - 2\Delta x + (\Delta x)^2) + 3 - 3\Delta x$$
$$= -5\Delta x + (\Delta x)^2 + 4 \quad \text{Simplify.}$$

$f(-1) = (-1)^2 - 3(-1)$ Find $f(-1)$.

$$= 4$$

$m = \displaystyle\lim_{\Delta x \to 0} \dfrac{-5\Delta x + (\Delta x)^2 + 4 - (4)}{\Delta x}$ Subtract and divide by Δx.

$= \displaystyle\lim_{\Delta x \to 0} \dfrac{-5\Delta x + (\Delta x)^2}{\Delta x}$ Add similar terms.

$= \displaystyle\lim_{\Delta x \to 0} \dfrac{\Delta x(-5 + \Delta x)}{\Delta x}$ Factor.

$= \displaystyle\lim_{\Delta x \to 0} -5 + \Delta x = -5$ Substitute 0 for Δx.

Thus the slope of the tangent to $f(x) = -x^2 - 3x$ at the point $(-1, 4)$ is -5.

Finding the Slope in General

If we need the slope of the tangent at several points on the curve $f(x)$, or if we want a formula for finding the slope anywhere, we do not replace x in the formula with a number.

EXAMPLE 2

Find the slope of the tangent to $f(x)$.
a) $f(x) = 3x^2 - 2x + 1$

b) $f(x) = \dfrac{1}{x + 1}$

SOLUTION 2

a) $f(x + \Delta x) = 3(x + \Delta x)^2 - 2(x + \Delta x) + 1$

Find $f(x + \Delta x)$.

$$= 3(x^2 + 2x\Delta x + (\Delta x)^2) - 2x - 2\Delta x + 1$$

Simplify.

$$= 3x^2 + 6x\Delta x + 3(\Delta x)^2 - 2x - 2\Delta x + 1$$

$$f(x) = 3x^2 - 2x + 1 \qquad\qquad \text{Find } f(x).$$

$$m = \lim_{\Delta x \to 0} \frac{3x^2 + 6x\Delta x + 3(\Delta x)^2 - 2x - 2\Delta x + 1 - (3x^2 - 2x + 1)}{\Delta x}$$

$$= \lim_{\Delta x \to 0} \frac{3x^2 + 6x\Delta x + 3(\Delta x)^2 - 2x - 2\Delta x + 1 - 3x^2 + 2x - 1}{\Delta x}$$

$$= \lim_{\Delta x \to 0} \frac{6x\Delta x + 3(\Delta x)^2 - 2\Delta x}{\Delta x}$$

$$= \lim_{\Delta x \to 0} \frac{\Delta x(6x + 3(\Delta x) - 2)}{\Delta x} \qquad\qquad \text{Factor.}$$

$$= \lim_{\Delta x \to 0} 6x + 3\Delta x - 2 \qquad\qquad \frac{\Delta x}{\Delta x} = 1$$

$$= 6x + 3(0) - 2 \qquad\qquad \text{Substitute 0 for } \Delta x.$$

$$= 6x - 2 \qquad\qquad \text{This is the slope of the tangent.}$$

b) $\quad f(x + \Delta x) = \dfrac{1}{(x + \Delta x) + 1} \qquad\qquad \text{Find } f(x + \Delta x).$

$$= \frac{1}{x + \Delta x + 1}$$

$$f(x) = \frac{1}{x + 1} \qquad\qquad \text{Find } f(x).$$

$$m = \lim_{\Delta x \to 0} \frac{\dfrac{1}{x + \Delta x + 1} - \dfrac{1}{x + 1}}{\Delta x} \qquad\qquad \text{Subtract and divide by } \Delta x.$$

$$= \lim_{\Delta x \to 0} \frac{\dfrac{x + 1 - (x + \Delta x + 1)}{(x + \Delta x + 1)(x + 1)}}{\Delta x} \qquad\qquad \text{Find a common denominator to subtract the fractions.}$$

$$= \lim_{\Delta x \to 0} \frac{\dfrac{x + 1 - x - \Delta x - 1}{(x + \Delta x + 1)(x + 1)}}{\dfrac{\Delta x}{1}} \qquad\qquad \text{Distribute the subtraction sign. Write } \Delta x \text{ as } \dfrac{\Delta x}{1}.$$

$$= \lim_{\Delta x \to 0} \frac{-\Delta x}{(x + \Delta x + 1)(x + 1)} \cdot \frac{1}{\Delta x}$$ Simplify the numerator and invert and multiply.

$$= \lim_{\Delta x \to 0} \frac{-1}{(x + \Delta x + 1)(x + 1)}$$ $\frac{\Delta x}{\Delta x} = 1$.

$$= \frac{-1}{(x + (0) + 1)(x + 1)}$$ Substitute 0 for Δx.

$$= \frac{-1}{(x + 1)(x + 1)} \quad \text{or} \quad \frac{-1}{(x + 1)^2}$$ This is the slope of the tangent.

Velocity

By examining change in the distance an object travels divided by the change in time, we can form the limit definition of velocity.

> **Velocity**
> If $s(t)$ is the distance an object travels, then the velocity of the object
> at time t is $\lim_{\Delta t \to 0} \dfrac{s(t + \Delta t) - s(t)}{\Delta t}$.

This formula is equivalent to our earlier formula for slope of the tangent, and can be evaluated in the same manner.

EXAMPLE 3

An object travels along a line so that its distance traveled after t seconds is $s(t) = \sqrt{2t + 1}$. Find its velocity after 5 seconds.

SOLUTION 3

We must find the velocity when $t = 5$.

$$s(5 + \Delta t) = \sqrt{2(5 + \Delta t) + 1}$$ Find $s(5 + \Delta t)$.

$$= \sqrt{10 + 2\Delta t + 1}$$ Simplify.

$$s(t) = \sqrt{2(5) + 1} = \sqrt{11}$$ Find $s(5)$.

$$\lim_{\Delta t \to 0} \frac{\sqrt{10 + 2\Delta t + 1} - \sqrt{11}}{\Delta t}$$ Subtract and divide by Δt.

To evaluate this limit, multiply by the conjugate of the numerator.

$$= \lim_{\Delta t \to 0} \frac{\sqrt{10 + 2\Delta t + 1} - \sqrt{11}}{\Delta t} \cdot \frac{\sqrt{10 + 2\Delta t + 1} + \sqrt{11}}{\sqrt{10 + 2\Delta t + 1} + \sqrt{11}}$$

$$= \lim_{\Delta t \to 0} \frac{10 + 2\Delta t + 1 - 11}{\Delta t \, (\sqrt{10 + 2\Delta t + 1} + \sqrt{11})}$$ Multiply the numerator. Leave the denominator in factored form.

$$= \lim_{\Delta t \to 0} \frac{2\Delta t}{\Delta t \, (\sqrt{10 + 2\Delta t + 1} + \sqrt{11})}$$ Combine similar terms.

$$= \lim_{\Delta t \to 0} \frac{2}{\sqrt{10 + 2\Delta t + 1} + \sqrt{11}}$$ $\dfrac{\Delta t}{\Delta t} = 1$.

$$= \frac{2}{\sqrt{10 + 2\,(0) + 1} + \sqrt{11}}$$ Substitute 0 for Δt.

$$= \frac{2}{\sqrt{11} + \sqrt{11}} = \frac{2}{2\sqrt{11}} = \frac{1}{\sqrt{11}}$$ Simplify the denominator.

Therefore, the velocity is $\dfrac{1}{\sqrt{11}}$ after 5 seconds, which would probably be written as $\dfrac{\sqrt{11}}{11}$.

3.2 THE DERIVATIVE

In previous sections we used a limit to find the slope of a tangent to a curve and to find velocity. These formulas are equivalent, and in general are defined to be the derivative.

The Derivative of a Function $f(x)$

The derivative of a function f at x is

$$f'(x) = \lim_{\Delta x \to 0} \frac{f(x + \Delta x) - f(x)}{\Delta x}$$

if this limit exists.

Notation

The following notation is used to signify a derivative of $f(x)$:

$f'(x)$ read f prime of x

$\dfrac{dy}{dx}$ read the derivative of y with respect to x

y' read y prime

$D_x(y)$

$\dfrac{d}{dx}(f(x))$

Derivative Shortcuts

The limit definition of a derivative is time-consuming. Fortunately, there are several shortcuts (proofs are available in any standard textbook). The rules that follow must be memorized.

Function	Derivative	Derivative Rules
$f(x) = 5$	$f'(x) = 0$	The derivative of a constant is 0.
$f(x) = x^4$	$f'(x) = 4x^3$	The derivative of x^n is nx^{n-1} (called the Power Rule).
$f(x) = 5x^3$	$f'(x) = 5(3x^2)$ $= 15x^2$	The derivative of a constant times a function is the constant times the derivative of the function.
$f(x) = x^2 + x^5$	$f'(x) = 2x + 5x^4$	The derivative of a sum or difference of functions is the sum or difference of the derivatives.

Note that rules for finding derivatives of products and quotients will be introduced in the next section.

EXAMPLE 4

Find $f'(x)$.

a) $f(x) = 4x^3 - 7x^2 + 2$

b) $f(x) = \sqrt[3]{x} + \dfrac{5}{\sqrt{x}}$

c) $f(x) = \dfrac{1}{5x^2}$

d) $f(x) = (x^2 + 1)(2x + 3)$

SOLUTION 4

a) $f'(x) = 4(3x^2) - 7(2x) + 0$ Find the derivative of each term.

$\qquad = 12x^2 - 14x$

b) First rewrite the terms to make use of the Power Rule:

$$f(x) = x^{1/3} + \dfrac{5}{x^{1/2}}$$

$$= x^{1/3} + 5x^{-1/2}$$

Now take the derivative of each term:

$$f'(x) = \dfrac{1}{3}x^{-2/3} + 5\left(-\dfrac{1}{2}x^{-3/2}\right) \qquad \dfrac{1}{3} - 1 = \dfrac{1}{3} - \dfrac{3}{3} = -\dfrac{2}{3}$$

$$-\dfrac{1}{2} - 1 = -\dfrac{1}{2} - \dfrac{2}{2} = -\dfrac{3}{2}$$

$$= \dfrac{1}{3}x^{-2/3} - \dfrac{5}{2}x^{-3/2} \qquad \text{Simplify.}$$

c) $f(x) = \dfrac{1}{5x^2} = \dfrac{1}{5}x^{-2}$ Rewrite the function.

$\qquad f'(x) = \dfrac{1}{5}(-2x^{-3})$ Use the Power Rule.

$\qquad = -\dfrac{2}{5}x^{-3}$ or $-\dfrac{2}{5x^3}$ Answer may be written in either form.

d) Before using the Power Rule and the rule for sums, we must multiply:

$$f(x) = (x^2 + 1)(2x + 3)$$

$$= 2x^3 + 3x^2 + 2x + 3 \qquad \text{Multiply.}$$

$$f'(x) = 2(3x^2) + 3(2x) + 2(1x^0) + 0 \quad \text{Use the Power Rule.}$$
$$= 6x^2 + 6x + 2$$

EXAMPLE 5

Find an equation of the tangent line to $f(x) = x^3 + 2x + 1$ at $(1, 4)$.

SOLUTION 5

Since the slope of the tangent line equals the derivative, find $f'(x)$.

$$f'(x) = 3x^2 + 2 \qquad\qquad m = f'(x).$$

We need the slope at $x = 1$.

$$f'(x) = 3(1)^2 + 2 = 5$$

Now use the point-slope form of a line:

$y - y_1 = m(x - x_1)$	Substitute $(x_1, y_1) = (1, 4)$
$y - 4 = 5(x - 1)$	and $m = 5$.
$y - 4 = 5x - 5$	Simplify.
$y = 5x - 1$	

3.3 THE PRODUCT AND QUOTIENT RULES

The Product Rule   When a function consists of a product that can be easily multiplied, it is usually faster to multiply first and then find the derivative. Otherwise, we'll use the Product Rule.

To Find the Derivative of $h(x) = f(x) \cdot g(x)$:

1. Find $f'(x)$ and $g'(x)$.
2. Set up the following: $f(x) \quad g(x)$
   $\qquad\qquad\qquad f'(x) \quad g'(x)$
3. $h'(x) = g(x) \cdot f'(x) + f(x)g'(x)$

EXAMPLE 6

Use the Product Rule to find $h'(x)$.

a) $h(x) = (x^2 + 1)(2x + 3)$

b) $h(x) = (x^2 - 2x + 1)(4x^2 - 9)$

SOLUTION 6

a) $x^2 + 1 \quad + \quad 2x + 3$ $f(x) = x^2 + 1 \quad g(x) = 2x + 3$

      $2x \qquad\qquad 2$ $f'(x) = 2x \quad g'(x) = 2$

$h'(x) = (2x + 3)(2x) + (x^2 + 1)(2)$ Use the Product Rule.

$$= 4x^2 + 6x + 2x^2 + 2 \qquad \text{Simplify.}$$

$$= 6x^2 + 6x + 2$$

Compare this answer to Example 4d.

b) $x^2 - 2x + 1 \quad + \quad 4x^2 - 9$ $f(x) = x^2 - 2x + 1$

    $2x - 2 \qquad\qquad 8x$ $g(x) = 4x^2 - 9$

                                  Find $f'(x)$ and $g'(x)$.

$h'(x) = (4x^2 - 9)(2x - 2) + (x^2 - 2x + 1)(8x)$

                                  Use the Product Rule.

$$= 8x^3 - 8x^2 - 18x + 18 + 8x^3 - 16x^2 + 8x$$

                                  Multiply.

$$= 16x^3 - 24x^2 - 10x + 18 \qquad \text{Simplify.}$$

The Quotient Rule

If a fraction consists of a constant in the numerator or denominator, it's faster to rewrite it and use the Power Rule (see Example 4c) or the Chain Rule (see Example 14b). Otherwise, we'll use the Quotient Rule.

To Find the Derivative of $h(x) = \dfrac{f(x)}{g(x)}$:

1. Find $f'(x)$ and $g'(x)$.
2. Set up the following: $f(x) \quad - \quad g(x)$

                           $f'(x) \qquad g'(x)$

3. $h'(x) = \dfrac{g(x)f'(x) - f(x)g'(x)}{[g(x)]^2}$

Note that the Quotient Rule uses a subtraction rather than addition between $g(x)f'(x)$ and $f(x)g'(x)$ and that the denominator is always the original denominator squared.

EXAMPLE 7

Use the Quotient Rule to find $h'(x)$.

a) $h(x) = \dfrac{2x+1}{4x-3}$

b) $h(x) = \dfrac{4x^3 - 2x^2 + 1}{x^2 - 9}$

SOLUTION 7

a) $2x+1$ $4x-3$ $f(x) = 2x+1.$

                                             $g(x) = 4x-3.$

       2 4 Find $f'(x)$ and $g'(x)$.

$h'(x) = \dfrac{(4x-3)\,(2) - (2x+1)\,(4)}{(4x-3)^2}$ Use the Quotient Rule.

$= \dfrac{8x - 6 - 8x - 4}{(4x-3)^2}$ Simplify.

$= \dfrac{-10}{(4x-3)^2}$ Combine similar terms.

b) $4x^3 - 2x^2 + 1$ $x^2 - 9$ State $f(x)$ and $g(x)$.

       $12x^2 - 4x$ $2x$ Find $f'(x)$ and $g'(x)$.

$h'(x) = \dfrac{(x^2-9)\,(12x^2-4x) - (4x^3 - 2x^2 + 1)\,(2x)}{(x^2-9)^2}$

Use the Quotient Rule.

$= \dfrac{12x^4 - 4x^3 - 108x^2 + 36x - 8x^4 + 4x^3 - 2x}{(x^2-9)^2}$

Simplify.

$= \dfrac{4x^4 - 108x^2 + 34x}{(x^2-9)^2}$ Combine similar terms.

Combining the Product and Quotient Rules

You may need both rules to work a problem if a product or quotient contains a product and/or quotient.

EXAMPLE 8

Find the derivative.

a) $h(x) = (\dfrac{2x+1}{4x-3}) \, (x^2+4x)$

b) $h(x) = \dfrac{(x^2-4x+2) \, (x^2+3)}{x^2-1}$

SOLUTION 8

a)

$\dfrac{2x+1}{4x-3}$ $\qquad +\qquad$ x^2+4x $\qquad\qquad$ Identify $f(x)$ and $g(x)$.

$\dfrac{-10}{(4x-3)^2}$ $\qquad\qquad\quad$ $2x+4$ $\qquad\qquad$ Find $f'(x)$ (see Example 7a) and $g'(x)$.

$h'(x) = (x^2+4x) \, (\dfrac{-10}{(4x-3)^2}) + (\dfrac{2x+1}{4x-3}) \, (2x+4)$

$\qquad\qquad\qquad\qquad\qquad\qquad$ Use the Product Rule.

$= \dfrac{-10x^2-40x}{(4x-3)^2} + \dfrac{4x^2+10x+4}{4x-3}$ $\qquad$ Multiply.

$= \dfrac{-10x^2-40x}{(4x-3)^2} + \dfrac{4x^2+10x+4}{4x-3} \cdot \dfrac{4x-3}{4x-3}$

$\qquad\qquad\qquad\qquad\qquad\qquad$ Use $(4x-3)^2$ as the LCD.

$= \dfrac{-10x^2-40x}{(4x-3)^2} + \dfrac{16x^3+28x^2-14x-12}{(4x-3)^2}$

$\qquad\qquad\qquad\qquad\qquad\qquad$ Multiply.

$= \dfrac{16x^3+18x^2-54x-12}{(4x-3)^2}$ $\qquad\qquad$ Add the numerators.

b) First find the derivative of $p(x) = (x^2 - 4x + 2)\,(x^2 + 3)$ using
the Product Rule.

$$x^2 - 4x + 2 \qquad + \qquad x^2 + 3 \qquad\qquad \text{Identify } f(x) \text{ and } g(x).$$
$$2x - 4 \qquad\qquad\qquad 2x \qquad\qquad \text{Find } f'(x) \text{ and } g'(x).$$

$$p'(x) = (x^2 + 3)\,(2x - 4) + (x^2 - 4x + 2)\,(2x)$$

Use the Product Rule.

$$= 2x^3 - 4x^2 + 6x - 12 + 2x^3 - 8x^2 + 4x \qquad \text{Multiply.}$$

$$= 4x^3 - 12x^2 + 10x - 12 \qquad\qquad \text{Combine similar terms.}$$

Now find $h'(x)$.

$$(x^2 - 4x + 2)\,(x^2 + 3) \qquad x^2 - 1 \qquad \text{Identify } f(x) \text{ and } g(x).$$
$$4x^3 - 12x^2 + 10x - 12 \qquad 2x \qquad \text{Find } f'(x) \text{ and } g'(x).$$

$$h'(x) =$$

$$\frac{(x^2 - 1)\,(4x^3 - 12x^2 + 10x - 12) - (x^2 - 4x + 2)\,(x^2 + 3)\,(2x)}{(x^2 - 1)^2}$$

Use the Quotient Rule.

$$= \frac{3x^5 - 4x^4 - 4x^3 + 4x^2 - 22x - 12}{(x^2 - 1)^2}$$

Multiply and combine
similar terms.

3.4 THE CHAIN RULE

The Chain Rule provides a method for finding derivatives of composite
functions.

The Chain Rule
If $y = (f \circ g)(x) = f(g(x))$, then $y' = f'(g(x))g'(x)$.

If we think of a composition as having an "inside" and an "outside",
then the Chain Rule says to multiply the derivative of the outside function

times the derivative of the inside function.
For example, to find the derivative of

$$y = \underbrace{(x^3 + 2)}^2$$
$$\text{inside function}$$

imagine covering up the inside function $x^3 + 2$:

$$y = (\rule{2cm}{0.3cm})^2$$

Then $y' = 2(\rule{2cm}{0.3cm})^1$ Find the derivative of the
outside function.

Now multiply times the derivative of the inside function:

$$y' = 2(\rule{2cm}{0.3cm})^1 \cdot D_x[x^3 + 2]$$

$$y' = 2(\rule{2cm}{0.3cm})^1 \cdot 3x^2$$

Now replace the inside function and simplify:
$$y' = 2(x^3 + 2)^1 \underbrace{(3x^2)}$$
$$\text{derivative of the inside function.}$$

$$= 6x^2(x^3 + 2)$$ Simplify the result.

EXAMPLE 9

Find each derivative.

a) $y = \sqrt{4 - x^2}$

b) $h(x) = 3x(x^2 - 6)^4$

c) $y = (\dfrac{x - 2}{x + 1})^3$

SOLUTION 9

a) $y = (4 - x^2)^{1/2}$ Rewrite the square root.

$$y' = \frac{1}{2}(4 - x^2)^{-1/2}(-2x)$$ Multiply times the
derivative of $4 - x^2$.

$$= -x(4 - x^2)^{-1/2}$$ Simplify.

$$= \frac{-x}{\sqrt{4 - x^2}}$$

b) $h(x) = 3x(x^2 - 6)^4$ involves a product of two functions

$3x$ $(x^2 - 6)^4$ Identify $f(x)$ and $g(x)$.

3 $4(x^2 - 6)^3(2x)$ Find $f'(x)$ and $g'(x)$.

$h'(x) = (x^2 - 6)^4(3) + 3x[4(x^2 - 6)^3(2x)]$

Use the Product Rule.

Rather than multiply, it will be easier to factor out the common factor $3(x^2 - 6)^3$:

$h'(x) = 3(x^2 - 6)^3[(x^2 - 6) + x(4)(2x)]$ Common factor.

$= 3(x^2 - 6)^3[x^2 - 6 + 8x^2]$ Simplify inside the brackets.

$= 3(x^2 - 6)^3(9x^2 - 6)$ Combine similar terms.

$= 9(x^2 - 6)^3(3x^2 - 2)$ $9x^2 - 6 = 3(3x^2 - 2)$.

c) $y = \left(\dfrac{x-2}{x+1}\right)^3$

$y' = 3\left(\dfrac{x-2}{x+1}\right)^2 \cdot D_x\left(\dfrac{x-2}{x+1}\right)$ Use the Chain Rule.

$= 3\left(\dfrac{x-2}{x+1}\right)^2\left[\dfrac{(x+1)(1) - (x-2)(1)}{(x+1)^2}\right]$

Use the Quotient Rule.

$= 3\left(\dfrac{x-2}{x+1}\right)^2\left[\dfrac{3}{(x+1)^2}\right]$ Simplify the numerator.

$= 3\dfrac{(x-2)^2}{(x+1)^2} \cdot \dfrac{3}{(x+1)^2}$ Use exponent laws to write

$\left(\dfrac{a}{b}\right)^2 = \dfrac{a^2}{b^2}$.

$$= \frac{9(x-2)^2}{(x+1)^4}$$

Add exponents:

$$(x+1)^2(x+1)^2 = (x+1)^4.$$

3.5 DERIVATIVES OF TRIGONOMETRIC FUNCTIONS

The derivatives of the trigonometric functions can now be stated using the Chain Rule.

Derivatives of the Trigonometric Functions

$D_x[\sin u] = (\cos u)u'$

$D_x[\cos u] = -(\sin u)u'$

$D_x[\tan u] = (\sec^2 u)u'$

$D_x[\csc u] = -(\csc u \cot u)u'$

$D_x[\sec u] = (\sec u \tan u)u'$

$D_x[\cot u] = -(\csc^2 u)u'$

Note in each case we must multiply by u', the derivative of the angle.

EXAMPLE 10

Find y'.

a) $y = \sin x^2$

b) $y = \cos(2x+1)$

c) $y = 3\tan \pi x$

SOLUTION 10

a) Let $u = x^2$. Then $u' = 2x$.

$y' = \cos(x^2)(2x)$ Multiply times u'.

$y' = 2x\cos x^2$ x^2 is the angle, and cannot be multiplied times the $2x$.

b) Let $u = 2x+1$. Then $u' = 2$.

$y' = -\sin(2x+1)(2)$ Multiply times u'.

$y' = -2\sin(2x+1)$ Simplify.

c) Let $u = \pi x$. Then $u' = \pi$.

$y' = 3(\sec^2 \pi x)(\pi)$ Multiply times u'.

$y' = 3\pi(\sec^2 \pi x)$

Using the Product and Quotient Rule

We can now use the Product and Quotient Rules on functions that involve one or more trigonometric functions.

EXAMPLE 11

Differentiate.

a) $y = x^3 \sin x^2$

b) $y = \sin x \tan x$

c) $y = \dfrac{1 - \sin x}{\cos x}$

SOLUTION 11

a) x^3 + $\sin x^2$ Identify $f(x)$ and $g(x)$.

   $3x^2$ $2x\cos x^2$ Find $f'(x)$ and $g'(x)$.

$y' = (\sin x^2)(3x^2) + (x^3)(2x\cos x^2)$ Use the Product Rule.

$= 3x^2 \sin x^2 + 2x^4 \cos x^2$

b) $\sin x$ + $\tan x$ Identify $f(x)$ and $g(x)$.

   $\cos x$ $\sec^2 x$ Find $f'(x)$ and $g'(x)$.

$y' = \tan x \cos x + \sin x \sec^2 x$ Use the Product Rule.

$= \dfrac{\sin x}{\cos x} \cdot \cos x + \sin x \sec^2 x$ Use an identity.

$= \sin x + \sin x \sec^2 x$ Simplify.

c) $1 - \sin x$ − $\cos x$ Identify $f(x)$ and $g(x)$.

   $-\cos x$ $-\sin x$ Find $f'(x)$ and $g'(x)$.

$y' = \dfrac{\cos x (-\cos x) - (1 - \sin x)(-\sin x)}{(\cos x)^2}$ Use the Quotient Rule.

$= \dfrac{\cos^2 x + \sin x - \sin^2 x}{\cos^2 x}$ Multiply.

$$= \frac{-\cos^2 x - \sin^2 x + \sin x}{\cos^2 x}$$ Change the order.

$$= \frac{-1 + \sin x}{\cos^2 x}$$ $-\cos^2 x - \sin^2 x =$
$-(\cos^2 x + \sin^2 x) = -(1).$

Differentiating Powers of Trigonometric Functions

The expression $\sin^2 x$ means $(\sin x)^2$. When differentiating powers of trigonometric functions, rewriting the power outside a set of parentheses will help remind you that a Chain Rule must be used. Study the examples that follow.

EXAMPLE 12

Find the derivatives.
a) $y = \sin^2 x$

b) $y = \sec^3 4x^2$

c) $y = 2\sqrt{\cos 3x}$

SOLUTION 12

a) $y = (\sin x)^2$ Rewrite the power outside parentheses.

$y' = 2(\sin x)^1 (\cos x)$ Use the Chain Rule.

$y' = 2\sin x \cos x \quad \text{or} \quad \sin 2x$ Simplify by using a double-angle identity.

b) $y = \left(\sec 4x^2 \right)^3$ Rewrite the power outside parentheses.

$y' = 3\left(\sec 4x^2 \right)^2 D\left[\sec 4x^2 \right]$ Use the Chain Rule.

$D\left[\sec 4x^2 \right] = \sec 4x^2 \tan 4x^2 (8x)$
So,
$y' = 3\left(\sec 4x^2 \right)^2 \sec 4x^2 \tan 4x^2 (8x)$ Find the derivative of $\sec 4x^2$.

$y' = 24x \sec^2 4x^2 \sec 4x^2 \tan 4x^2$ Simplify.

$y' = 24x \sec^3 4x^2 \tan 4x^2$ Use exponent laws to multiply the $(\sec^2 u)(\sec u) = \sec^3 u.$

c) $y = 2(\cos 3x)^{1/2}$ Rewrite the square root as a power.

$y' = 2\left[\dfrac{1}{2}(\cos 3x)^{-1/2}\right]D(\cos 3x)$ Use the Chain Rule.

$D(\cos 3x) = -\sin 3x(3)$ Find the derivative of $\cos 3x$.

So,

$y' = (\cos 3x)^{-1/2}(-\sin 3x(3))$ Multiply.

$y' = \dfrac{-3\sin 3x}{\sqrt{\cos 3x}}$ Rewrite.

3.6 Higher-Order Derivatives

We have used the first derivative to find the slope of a tangent to a curve and to find velocity.

We will use higher-order derivatives to find acceleration and certain features of graphs. Higher-order derivatives are found by taking derivatives of derivatives. For example, if $f(x) = x^4$,

$f'(x) = 4x^3$	First derivative
$f''(x) = 12x^2$	Second derivative
$f'''(x) = 24x$	Third derivative
$f^{(4)}(x) = 24$	Fourth derivative
$f^{(5)}(x) = 0$	Fifth derivative

The following table contains some of the notation associated with higher order derivatives.

Notation for Derivatives				
First Derivative	$f'(x)$	y'	$D_x(y)$	$\dfrac{d}{dx}[f(x)]$

Notation for Derivatives				
Second Derivative	$f''(x)$	y''	$D_x^2(y)$	$\dfrac{d^2}{dx}[f(x)]$
Third Derivative	$f'''(x)$	y'''	$D_x^3(y)$	$\dfrac{d^3}{dx}[f(x)]$

EXAMPLE 13

Find y''.

a) $y = 6x^3 + 3x^2 - 5x + 2$

b) $y = \sin 2x$

SOLUTION 13

a) $y' = 18x^2 + 6x - 5$ Find y'.

    $y'' = 36x + 6$ Find y''.

b) $y' = \cos 2x\,(2)$ Find y'.

    $y' = 2\cos 2x$ Simplify.

    $y'' = 2\,[-\sin 2x\,(2)]$ Find y''.

    $y'' = -4\sin 2x$ Simplify.

Using the Product and Quotient Rules

Higher-order derivatives involving the Product and Quotient Rules can get very large very fast. Simplify each derivative as much as possible before finding the next derivative.

EXAMPLE 14

Find the second derivative.

a) $y = x(x^2 - 1)^3$

b) $y = \dfrac{2x - 1}{x + 3}$

SOLUTION 14

a) x $+$ $(x^2 - 1)^3$ Identify $f(x)$ and $g(x)$.

    1 $3(x^2 - 1)^2(2x)$ Find $f'(x)$ and $g'(x)$ using the Chain Rule.

$$y' = (x^2 - 1)^3 (1) + x(3)(x^2 - 1)^2 (2x) \quad \text{Use the Product Rule.}$$

$$y' = (x^2 - 1)^2 [(x^2 - 1) + x(3)(2x)] \quad \text{Common factor.}$$

$$y = (x^2 - 1)^2 (7x^2 - 1) \qquad\qquad \text{Combine similar terms.}$$

$$(x^2 - 1)^2 \quad \times \quad + \quad 7x^2 - 1 \qquad \text{Identify } f(x) \text{ and } g(x).$$

$$2(x^2 - 1)^1 (2x) \qquad\qquad 14x \qquad\qquad \text{Find } f'(x) \text{ and } g'(x).$$

$$y'' = (7x^2 - 1)(2)(x^2 - 1)(2x) + (x^2 - 1)^2 (14x)$$
Use the Product Rule.

$$y'' = 2x(x^2 - 1)[(7x^2 - 1)(2) + (x^2 - 1)(7)]$$
Common factor.

$$y'' = 2x(x^2 - 1)[14x^2 - 2 + 7x^2 - 7] \quad \text{Multiply.}$$

$$y'' = 2x(x^2 - 1)(21x^2 - 9) \qquad\qquad \text{Combine similar terms.}$$

$$y'' = 6x(x^2 - 1)(7x^2 - 3) \qquad\qquad 21x^2 - 9 = 3(7x^2 - 3).$$

b) $2x - 1 \quad - \quad x + 3 \qquad\qquad$ Identify $f(x)$ and $g(x)$.

$\quad 2 \qquad\qquad\quad 1 \qquad\qquad\qquad$ Find $f'(x)$ and $g'(x)$.

$$y' = \frac{(x+3)(2) - (2x-1)(1)}{(x+3)^2} \qquad \text{Use the Quotient Rule.}$$

$$y' = \frac{2x + 6 - 2x + 1}{(x+3)^2} \qquad\qquad \text{Multiply.}$$

$$y' = \frac{7}{(x+3)^2}$$

y'' can be found by using the Quotient Rule again or by rewriting y' as $y' = 7(x+3)^{-2}$ and using the Power Rule and Chain Rule. We'll proceed with the Power Rule:

$$y'' = 7\left[-2(x+3)^{-3}(1)\right]$$ Use the Power Rule.

$$y'' = -14(x+3)^{-3}$$ Multiply.

$$y'' = \frac{-14}{(x+3)^3}$$ Write the answer using positive exponents.

Trigonometric Functions and Higher-order Derivatives

We can also find higher-order derivatives of the trigonometric functions. To review the rules of the first derivatives, see section 3.5.

EXAMPLE 15

Find the indicated derivative.

a) $\dfrac{d^3y}{dx^3}$ if $\dfrac{dy}{dx} = \sin x$

b) $D_x^2(y)$ if $y = x\cos x$

SOLUTION 15

a) $\dfrac{d^3y}{dx^3}$ is notation for the third derivative.

$$\frac{dy}{dx} = \sin x$$ Given the first derivative.

$$\frac{d^2y}{dx^2} = \cos x$$ Find the second derivative.

$$\frac{d^3y}{dx^3} = -\sin x$$ Find the third derivative.

b) $D_x^2(y)$ is the second derivative. Since $x\cos x$ is a product we must use the Product Rule.

x	$+$	$\cos x$	Identify $f(x)$ and $g(x)$.
1		$-\sin x$	Find $f'(x)$ and $g'(x)$.

$$D_x(y) = (\cos x)(1) + (x)(-\sin x)$$ Find the first derivative.

$$D_x(y) = \cos x - x\sin x$$ Simplify.

$D_x(y)$ is a difference of two functions, so we take the derivative of each term. However, one of the terms is a product, whose derivative is found using the Product Rule.

$$D_x{}^2(y) = D_x(\cos x) - D_x(x\sin x)$$ $x \ + \ \sin x$

$$D_x{}^2(y) = -\sin x - [(\sin x)(1) + x\cos x]$$ $1 \qquad \cos x$

$$D_x{}^2(y) = -\sin x - \sin x - x\cos x$$ Distribute.

$$D_x{}^2(y) = -2\sin x - x\cos x$$ Combine similar terms.

3.7 IMPLICIT DIFFERENTIATION

The functions we have differentiated in this chapter have been solved *explicitly* for y. However, not all functions will be written (or even *can* be) written explicitly. When a function is written *implicitly*, we treat x and y as functions, and use the Chain Rule to write each derivative of y as y '.

Using the Chain Rule on y

EXAMPLE 16

Differentiate with respect to x.

a) x^3

b) y^3

c) x^3y^3

SOLUTION 16

a) $D_x[x^3] = 3x^2 \cdot D_x[x]$ Use the Chain Rule.

$\qquad = 3x^2(1)$ $D_x[x] = 1$.

$\qquad = 3x^2$ Simplify.

b) $D_x[y^3] = 3y^2 \cdot D_x[y]$ Use the Chain Rule.

$\qquad = 3y^2 \cdot y'$ $D_x[y] = y'$.

$\qquad = 3y^2y'$ Simplify.

c) $D_x [x^3 y^3]$ involves a product of x^3 and y^3. We use the Product Rule.

x^3 y^3 Identify f and g.

$3x^2$ $3y^2 y'$ Find f' and g'.

$$D_x [x^3 y^3] = y^3 (3x^2) + x^3 (3y^2 y')$$ Use the Product Rule.
$$= 3x^2 y^3 + 3x^3 y^2 y'$$ Simplify.

Implicit Differentiation

The following rules will help you find a derivative using implicit differentiation. Keep in mind that the goal is to solve for y'.

Finding a First Derivative with Implicit Differentiation
1. Find the derivative of both sides of the equation.
2. Collect all terms involving y' on the left side of the equation, and all other terms on the right side of the equation.
3. Factor out y' on the left side.
4. Divide both sides of the equation by the coefficient of y'.

EXAMPLE 17

Find y'.

a) $x^3 + x^3 y^3 + y^3 = 6$

b) $x^2 y^2 - y = 6x$

c) $x \sin y = 1$

SOLUTION 17

a) $D_x [x^3 + x^3 y^3 + y^3] = D_x[6]$ Find the derivative of both sides.

$$3x^2 + 3x^2 y^3 + 3x^3 y^2 y' + 3y^2 y' = 0$$ See Example 16 for the left side. The derivative of a constant is 0.

$$3x^3 y^2 y' + 3y^2 y' = -3x^2 - 3x^2 y^3$$ Move all terms with y' to the left, all other terms to the right.

$$y'\,(3x^3y^2 + 3y^2) = -3x^2 - 3x^2y^3$$

Factor out y'.

$$y' = \frac{-3x^2 - 3x^2y^3}{3x^3y^2 + 3y^2}$$

Divide both sides by the coefficient of y'.

$$y' = \frac{-x^2 - x^2y^3}{x^3y^2 + y^2}$$

Factor out $\frac{3}{3}$ and reduce.

b) $D_x\,[x^2y^2 - y] = D_x[6x]$

Find the derivative of both sides.

$$y^2\,(2x) + x^2\,(2yy') - y' = 6$$

$x^2 \quad \pm \quad y^2$

$2x \qquad 2yy'$

$$2x^2yy' - y' = 6 - 2xy^2$$

Move all terms with y' to the left, all other terms to the right.

$$y'\,(2x^2y - 1) = 6 - 2xy^2$$

Factor out y'.

$$y' = \frac{6 - 2xy^2}{2x^2y - 1}$$

Divide both sides by the coefficient of y'.

$$y' = \frac{-x^2\,(y^3 + 1)}{y^2\,(x^3 + 1)}$$

Simplify by factoring.

c) $D_x\,[x\sin y] = D_x[1]$

Find the derivatives of both sides.

$$\sin y + x\cos y\,y' = 0$$

$x \quad + \quad \sin y$

$1 \qquad (\cos y)(y')$

Move all terms with y' to the left, all other terms to the right.

$$x\cos y\,y' = -\sin y$$

Divide both sides by the coefficient of y'.

$$y' = \frac{-\sin y}{x\cos y}$$

$$y' = -\frac{1}{x}\tan y$$

Use trigonometric identities

to write $\dfrac{\sin y}{\cos y} = \tan y$.

Slope of a Tangent Line   Recall from sections 1 and 2 that the slope of a tangent line to a curve is the first derivative. If the equation of the curve is stated implicitly, find the slope of the tangent using implicit differentiation.

EXAMPLE 18

Find the slope of the tangent line at the indicated point.

a) $x^2 + 4y^2 = 100$ at $(-8, 3)$

b) $4x^2 - 3y^2 + 8x + 16 = 0$ at $(0, \dfrac{4}{\sqrt{3}})$

SOLUTION 18

a) Since the slope of the tangent line equals the first derivative, find y'.

$$D_x\,[x^2 + 4y^2] = D_x[100]$$ Find the derivative of both sides.

$$2x + 8yy' = 0$$ $D_x[\,4y^2\,] = 8yD_x[y]$
$= 8yy'$

$$8yy' = -2x$$ Isolate y'.

$$y' = \frac{-2x}{8y}$$ Divide both sides by $8y$.

$$y' = -\frac{x}{4y}$$ y' is the slope of the tangent.

Find the slope at $(-8, 3)$:

$$y' = -\frac{(-8)}{4\,(3)}$$ Substitute $x = -8$ and $y = 3$.

$$y' = \frac{2}{3}$$ Reduce.

b) $D_x\,[4x^2 - 3y^2 + 8x + 16] = D_x[0]$ Find the derivative of both sides.

$$8x - 6yy' + 8 = 0$$ $D_x\,[-3y^2] = -6y \cdot D_x[y]$
$= -6yy'$.

$$-6yy' = -8x - 8$$ Isolate y'.

$$y' = \frac{-8x - 8}{-6y}$$

Divide both sides by $-6y$.

$$y' = \frac{4x + 4}{3y}$$

y' is the slope of the tangent.

Find the slope at $(0, \frac{4}{\sqrt{3}})$:

$$y' = \frac{4(0) + 4}{3(\frac{4}{\sqrt{3}})}$$

Substitute $x = 0$, $y = \frac{4}{\sqrt{3}}$.

$$y' = \frac{4}{\frac{12}{\sqrt{3}}} = 4 \cdot \frac{\sqrt{3}}{12} = \frac{\sqrt{3}}{3}$$

Simplify.

EXAMPLE 19

Find the equation of the tangent line at the indicated point.

a) $x^2 + 4y^2 = 100$ at $(-8, 3)$

b) $4x^2 - 3y^2 + 8x + 16 = 0$ at $(0, \frac{4}{\sqrt{3}})$

SOLUTION 19

a)   We have already found the slope of the tangent at $(-8, 3)$ in Example 18a.

Use the point-slope formula to find the equation of the tangent line.

$$y - y_1 = m(x - x_1)$$

Write the point-slope formula.

$$y - 3 = \frac{2}{3}(x - (-8))$$

Substitute $y_1 = 3$, $m = \frac{2}{3}$, $x_1 = -8$.

$$y - 3 = \frac{2}{3}(x + 8)$$

Simplify.

$$y = \frac{2}{3}x + \frac{25}{3}$$

$\frac{2}{3} \cdot 8 + 3 = \frac{16}{3} + \frac{9}{3} = \frac{25}{3}$

b) $y - y_1 = m(x - x_1)$

Write the point-slope formula.

$$y - \frac{4}{\sqrt{3}} = \frac{\sqrt{3}}{3}(x - 0)$$

Substitute $y_1 = \frac{4}{\sqrt{3}}$,

$$m = \frac{\sqrt{3}}{3}, \, x_1 = 0.$$

$$y = \frac{\sqrt{3}}{3}x + \frac{4}{\sqrt{3}}$$

Solve for y.

or

$$y = \frac{\sqrt{3}x + 4\sqrt{3}}{3}$$

Answer may be written in this form.

Higher-order Derivatives Using Implicit Differentiation

When finding higher-order derivatives, it may be possible to replace y' with its equivalent and/or the original equation with its equivalent to help simplify the result. The example below uses both types of substitution to simplify the answer.

EXAMPLE 20

Find y'' if $x^2 + y^2 = 9$.

SOLUTION 20

$$D_x[x^2 + y^2] = D_x[9]$$

Find the derivative of both sides.

$$2x + 2yy' = 0$$

$D_x[y^2] = 2yD_x[y]$
$= 2yy'$.

$$2yy' = -2x$$
$$y' = -\frac{2x}{2y} = -\frac{x}{y}$$

Isolate y'.

Divide both sides by $2y$ and reduce.

To find y'', we will use the Quotient Rule.

$$
\begin{array}{ccc}
-x & \diagdown & y \\
-1 & \diagup & y'
\end{array}
$$

Identify f and g.

Find f' and g'.

$$y'' = \frac{y(-1) - (-x)(y')}{y^2}$$

Use the Quotient Rule.

$$= \frac{-y + xy'}{y^2}$$

Simplify.

$$= \frac{-y + x\left(-\frac{x}{y}\right)}{y^2}$$

Substitute $y' = -\frac{x}{y}$.

$$= \frac{-y - \frac{x^2}{y}}{y^2} \qquad \text{Simplify.}$$

$$= \frac{-y^2 - x^2}{y^3} \qquad \text{Multiply by } \frac{y}{y}.$$

$$= -\frac{(y^2 + x^2)}{y^3} \qquad \text{Factor out } -1.$$

$$= \frac{-(9)}{y^3} \qquad \text{Use } x^2 + y^2 = 9.$$

$$= -\frac{9}{y^3} \qquad \text{Final answer.}$$

In this chapter we introduced the limit definition of a derivative and various shortcuts to find derivatives of sums and differences, products, quotients, and compositions. We also used implicit differentiation to find y' for functions that were not solved for y (implicit functions). We used derivatives to find the slope of the tangent line to a curve, and to find velocity.

Practice Exercises

1. Use the limit definition of a derivative to find each derivative.

a) $f(x) = x^2 - 3x$

b) $f(x) = \sqrt{x-4}$

2. Find each derivative.

a) $y = \pi$

b) $y = 4x^3 - 7x^2 + 2x + 1$

c) $y = (3x - 1)(2x + 5)$

3. Use the Product Rule to find each derivative.

a) $y = (3x + 1)(4x - 6)$

b) $y = (x^2 + 2)(3x^2 - 5)$

c) $y = \sqrt{x}(2x - 1)$

4. Use the Quotient Rule to find each derivative.

a) $\dfrac{x^2 - 2x - 4}{x - 1}$

b) $\dfrac{3x - 2}{\sqrt{x}}$

5. Differentiate.

a) $y = (4x - 6)^3$

b) $y = \sqrt{x^2 - 2x + 1}$

c) $y = \sin^2 x$

6. Find $f'(x)$.

a) $f(x) = (2x + 1)^3 (x - 1)$

b) $f(x) = \dfrac{2x}{\sqrt{x^2 + 1}}$

c) $f(x) = \left(\dfrac{2x - 1}{x + 6}\right)^3$

7. Find $\dfrac{dy}{dx}$.

a) $y = \tan 2x$

b) $y = 5\sin\pi x + 2\cos 3x$

c) $y = \sec(3x)^2$

d) $y = \dfrac{\sin x}{\sec x + 1}$

8. Find the indicated derivative.

a) y'' if $y = 6x^2 + 4x - 2$

b) $D_x^2(y)$ if $y = 4x^{2/3}$

c) $\dfrac{d^3 y}{dx}$ if $y = \cos 2x$

9. Use implicit differentiation to find y'.

a) $x^2 + y^2 = 36$

b) $2x^2 + 4xy - y^2 = 9$

c) $x^2 \cos y = \sin x$

10. Find the equation of the tangent line at the given point.

a) $y = 4x^2 + 2x$ at $(3, 42)$

b) $y = \sin 3x$ at $\left(\dfrac{\pi}{3}, 0\right)$

Answers

1. a) $2x - 3$

    b) $\dfrac{1}{2\sqrt{x-4}}$

2. a) 0

    b) $12x^2 - 14x + 2$

    c) $12x + 13$

3. a) $24x - 14$

    b) $12x^3 + 2x$

    c) $\dfrac{6x - 1}{2\sqrt{x}}$

4. a) $\dfrac{x^2 - 2x + 6}{(x-1)^2}$

    b) $\dfrac{3x + 2}{2x^{3/2}}$

5. a) $12(4x - 6)^2$

    b) $\dfrac{x - 1}{\sqrt{x^2 - 2x + 1}}$

    c) $2\sin x \cos x$ or $\sin 2x$

6. a) $(2x + 1)^2 (8x - 5)$

    b) $\dfrac{2}{(x^2 + 1)^{3/2}}$

    c) $\dfrac{39(2x - 1)^2}{(x + 6)^4}$

7. a) $2\sec^2 2x$

    b) $5\pi \cos \pi x - 6\sin 3x$

    c) $18x \sec(3x)^2 \tan(3x)^2$

    d) $\dfrac{1 + \cos x - \tan^2 x}{(\sec x + 1)^2}$

8. a) 12

    b) $-\dfrac{8}{9}x^{-4/3}$

    c) $8\sin 2x$

9. a) $-\dfrac{x}{y}$

    b) $\dfrac{2x + 2y}{y - 2x}$

    c) $\dfrac{2x\cos y - \cos x}{x^2 \sin y}$

10. a) $y - 42 = 26(x - 3)$

    b) $y = -3x + \pi$

4

Applications of Derivatives

---

*I*n this chapter we will use derivatives to solve word problems and to analyze features of graphs. We will solve related rates problems, that is, problems in which variables change over time, and maximum and minimum problems.

4.1 RELATED RATES

Related rates problems involve one or more variables that change over time. Since the derivatives in these problems will be taken with respect to time, rather than with respect to *x*, we will use implicit differentiation (see section 3.7). Thus the statement
"the radius increases at a rate of 5 feet per second"
would be translated symbolically as

$$\frac{dr}{dt} = 5 \text{ feet/sec}$$

where *r* is the length of the radius.

EXAMPLE 1

Translate each statement into symbols.

a) The radius of a sphere is increasing at a rate of 10 feet per second.

b) The height of a cone is decreasing at a rate 6 inches per second

c) The angle of elevation is increasing at a rate of 12 radians per second.

SOLUTION 1

a) Let r = radius of the sphere

   Then $\dfrac{dr}{dt}$ = the rate of change of the radius.

   The statement translates as $\dfrac{dr}{dt} = 10$ feet/sec

b) Let h = height of the cone

   Then $\dfrac{dh}{dt}$ = the rate of change of the height.

   The statement translates as $\dfrac{dh}{dt} = -6$ in/sec where the negative indicates a decrease.

c) Let θ = the angle of elevation.

   Then $\dfrac{d\theta}{dt}$ = the rate of change of the angle.

   The statement translates as $\dfrac{d\theta}{dt} = 12$ rad/sec

Implicit Differentiation and Related Rates

Because related rates involve change with respect to time, we will need implicit differentiation. Study the following example.

EXAMPLE 2

Differentiate each equation with respect to t.

a) $A = \pi r^2$

b) $V = \pi r^3$

c) $V = \dfrac{1}{3}\pi r^2 h$

d) $\tan\theta = cy$ where c is a constant

SOLUTION 2

a) $A = \pi r^2$ Given equation.

   $\dfrac{dA}{dt} = \pi\,(2r^1)\dfrac{dr}{dt}$ Find the derivative of each side.

   $\dfrac{dA}{dt} = 2\pi r\dfrac{dr}{dt}$ Simplify.

b) $V = \pi r^3$ Given equation.

   $\dfrac{dV}{dt} = \pi\,(3r^2)\dfrac{dr}{dt}$ Find the derivative of each side.

$$\frac{dV}{dt} = 3\pi r^2 \frac{dr}{dt}$$

Simplify.

c) $V = \frac{1}{3}\pi r^2 h$

Given equation.

$$\frac{dV}{dt} = \frac{1}{3}\pi\left[h 2r\frac{dr}{dt} + r^2\frac{dh}{dt}\right]$$

Product Rule.

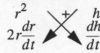

$$\frac{dV}{dt} = \frac{1}{3}\pi\left[2hr\frac{dr}{dt} + r^2\frac{dh}{dt}\right]$$

Simplify.

d) $\tan\theta = cy$

Given equation.

$$\sec^2\theta\frac{d\theta}{dt} = c\frac{dy}{dt}$$

Find the derivative of each side.

Solving Related Rates Problems

Some general guidelines for setting up related rates problems are:
1. Find an equation that describes the relationship between the variables.
2. Express the given information symbolically, taking care to represent each rate as a derivative with respect to time. Identify what you are looking for using symbols.
3. Differentiate both sides of the equation from step 1 with respect to time.
4. Substitute given information to find whatever is required.

Related Rates and Area

EXAMPLE 3

Oil spills into a lake in a circular pattern. If the radius of the circle increases at a rate of 2 feet per second, how fast is the area of the spill increasing at the end of 30 minutes?

SOLUTION 3

$A = \pi r^2$

Use the formula for the area of a circle.

$\frac{dr}{dt} = 2$ feet/second

Radius increases at a rate of 2 ft/sec.

Find $\frac{dA}{dt}$ when $t = 30$ minutes

Identify what you're looking for.

$$\frac{dA}{dt} = 2\pi r \frac{dr}{dt}$$ Find the derivative with
                                                                          respect to time.

When $t = 30$ minutes $= 30(60)$ seconds $= 1800$ seconds,

$r = 2(1800) = 3600$ feet   ft/sec times seconds = feet.

$$\frac{dA}{dt} = 2\pi\,(3600\,\text{ft})\,(2\,\text{ft/sec})$$ Substitute values for r and
                                                                          $\frac{dr}{dt}$.

$$\frac{dA}{dt} = 14,400\pi\ \text{ft}^2/\text{sec}$$ Simplify.

Related Rates and   **EXAMPLE 4**
Volume   Air is being pumped into a spherical balloon at a rate of 6 cubic inches per
                          minute. Find the rate of change of the radius when the radius is 1.5
                          inches.
                          SOLUTION 4

$$V = \frac{4}{3}\pi r^3$$ Use the formula for the
                                                                          volume of a sphere.

$$\frac{dV}{dt} = 6\,\text{in}^3/\text{min}$$ Volume increases at a rate
                                                                          of 6 in^3/min.

Find $\frac{dr}{dt}$ when $r = 1.5$ in   Identify what you're
                                                                          looking for.

$$\frac{dV}{dt} = \frac{4}{3}\pi\,(3r^2)\,\frac{dr}{dt}$$ Find the derivative with
                                                                          respect to time.

$$\frac{dV}{dt} = 4\pi r^2 \frac{dr}{dt}$$ Simplify.

$$6\ \text{in}^3/\text{min} = 4\pi\,(1.5\,\text{in})^2 \frac{dr}{dt}$$ Substitute the given
                                                                          information.

$$6\ \text{in}^3/\text{min} = 9\pi\ \text{in}^2 \frac{dr}{dt}$$ Simplify.

$$\frac{6\,\text{in}^3/\text{min}}{9\pi\,\text{in}^2} = \frac{dr}{dt}$$ Solve for $\frac{dr}{dt}$.

$\dfrac{2}{3\pi}$ in/min $= \dfrac{dr}{dt}$ Simplify.

Thus the radius is increasing at a rate of $\dfrac{2}{3\pi}$ inches per minute.

Related Rates and the Pythagorean Theorem

EXAMPLE 5

A 13 foot ladder is leaning against the wall of a house. The base of the ladder slides away from the wall at a rate of 0.5 feet per second. How fast is the top of the ladder moving down the wall when the base is 12 feet from the wall?

SOLUTION 5

A sketch will prove useful here.

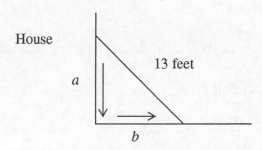

If we label the lengths as shown,

$$13^2 = a^2 + b^2$$ Use the Pythagorean theorem with $c = 13$.

$$\dfrac{db}{dt} = 0.5 \text{ ft/sec}$$ The base slides away at a rate of 0.5 ft/sec.

Find $\dfrac{da}{dt}$ when $b = 12$ Identify what you're looking for.

$$0 = 2a\dfrac{da}{dt} + 2b\dfrac{db}{dt}$$ Find the derivative with respect to time. The derivative of a constant is 0.

$$0 = 2a\dfrac{da}{dt} + 2b\,(0.5\,\text{ft/sec})$$ Substitute the given rate.

At this point there are still too many variables to solve for $\frac{da}{dt}$. We can find a when $b = 12$ feet and $c = 13$ feet:

$$c^2 = a^2 + b^2$$ Pythagorean theorem.

$$13^2 = a^2 + 12^2$$ Substitute for c and b.

$$25 = a^2$$ Solve for a.

$$a = 5 \text{ feet}$$

Then

$$0 = 2(5 \text{ feet})\frac{da}{dt} + 2(12 \text{ feet})(0.5 \text{ ft/sec})$$ Substitute the given and found values.

$$0 = 10 \text{ feet}\frac{da}{dt} + 12 \text{ ft}^2/\text{sec}$$ Simplify.

$$\frac{-12 \text{ ft}^2/\text{sec}}{10 \text{ ft}} = \frac{da}{dt}$$ Solve for $\frac{da}{dt}$.

$$-1.2 \text{ ft/sec} = \frac{da}{dt}$$

Thus, the top of the ladder is sliding down (note the negative sign in our answer) at a rate of 1.2 feet per second.

Related Rates and Angles

EXAMPLE 6

A weather balloon is released 50 feet from an observer. It rises at a rate of 8 feet per second. How fast is the angle of elevation changing when the balloon is 50 feet high?

SOLUTION 6

A sketch will prove useful here.

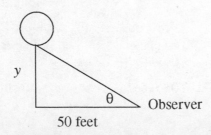

$$\tan\theta = \frac{y}{50}$$

Use the tangent to relate the angle of elevation to the given measures.

$$\frac{dy}{dt} = 8 \text{ ft/sec}$$

The balloon rises at a rate of 8 ft/sec.

Find $\frac{d\theta}{dt}$ when $y = 50$ feet

Identify what you are looking for.

$$\sec^2\theta \frac{d\theta}{dt} = \frac{1}{50}\frac{dy}{dt}$$

Find the derivative with respect to time.

$$\sec^2\theta \frac{d\theta}{dt} = \frac{1}{50}(8 \text{ ft/sec})$$

Substitute $\frac{dy}{dt}$.

$$\sec^2\theta \frac{d\theta}{dt} = \frac{4}{25} \text{ ft/sec}$$

Simplify.

We cannot solve for $\frac{d\theta}{dt}$ because we still have an unknown quantity, $\sec^2\theta$.

But, when $y = 50$ feet, $\tan\theta = \frac{50}{50}$ so $\tan\theta = 1$. Thus, $\theta = \frac{\pi}{4}$ radians.

$$\sec^2\left(\frac{\pi}{4}\right)\frac{d\theta}{dt} = \frac{4}{25}$$

Substitute $\frac{\pi}{4}$ for θ.

$$(\sqrt{2})^2\frac{d\theta}{dt} = \frac{4}{25}$$

$\sec\frac{\pi}{4} = \sqrt{2}$.

$$\frac{d\theta}{dt} = \frac{4}{25}\cdot\frac{1}{2}$$

Solve for $\frac{d\theta}{dt}$.

$$\frac{d\theta}{dt} = \frac{2}{25} \text{ rad/sec}$$

Thus the angle of elevation is increasing at a rate of $\frac{2}{25}$ radians per second.

4.2 DIFFERENTIALS

Finding Differentials   The differential, dy, is defined as the derivative $f'(x)$ times dx. Finding dy is straightforward.

> **To Find the Differential dy:**
> 1. Find $f'(x)$ (the derivative).
> 2. Multiply by dx. Leave dx in the answer.

EXAMPLE 7

Find dy for each function.

a) $y = 6x^3 - 2x^2 + 3x$

b) $y = \sqrt{2x+1}$

c) $y = x^2 \sin x$

SOLUTION 7

a) $y' = 18x^2 - 4x + 3$ Find y'.

   $dy = (18x^2 - 4x + 3)\,dx$ Multiply y' times dx.

b) $y = (2x+1)^{1/2}$ Rewrite the square root
                                           as a fractional exponent.

   $y' = \dfrac{1}{2}(2x+1)^{-1/2}(2)$ Use the Chain Rule to
                                           find y'.

   $dy = (2x+1)^{-1/2}\,dx$ Multiply y' times dx.

c) $y' = \sin x\,(2x) + x^2 \cos x$ $\begin{array}{cc} x^2 & +\quad \sin x \\ 2x & \diagdown\quad \cos x \end{array}$

   $dy = [2x\sin x + x^2\cos x]\,dx$ Multiply y' times dx.

The Differential as an Approximation   We can demonstrate the relationship between dx, Δx, dy and Δy graphically as follows:

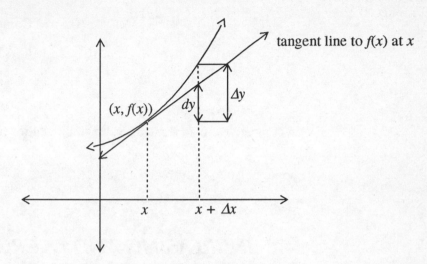

tangent line to $f(x)$ at x

$(x, f(x))$ dy Δy

x $x + \Delta x$

Thus Δy represents the actual change in y values along the curve $f(x)$, and dy represents the change along the tangent line. We can use dy to approximate Δy, especially for small increments in x (that is, when Δx is small).

Differentials as Approximations
$f(x + \Delta x) \approx f(x) + dy$

To approximate $f(x + \Delta x)$:
1. Identify $f(x)$.
2. Identify x and Δx.
3. Find $dy = f'(x)dx$.
4. Compute $f(x) + f'(x)\Delta x$.

EXAMPLE 8

Use differentials to approximate $\sqrt{9.6}$.

SOLUTION 8

We are interested in the square root of a number, so

$$f(x) = \sqrt{x} = x^{1/2} \qquad \text{Identify } f(x).$$

We know

$$f(9) = \sqrt{9} = 3, \text{ so}$$

$$f(9 + 0.6) \approx f(9) + dy \qquad x = 9 \text{ and } \Delta x = 0.6$$

$$dy = f'(x)dx$$ Definition of *dy*.

$$dy = \frac{1}{2}x^{-1/2}\,dx$$ Multiply derivative times *dx*.

$$f(9 + 0.6) \approx f(9) + \frac{1}{2}(9)^{-1/2}(0.6)$$ Compute $f(x) + f'(x)\Delta x$.

$$f(9 + 0.6) \approx 3 + \frac{1}{2} \cdot \frac{1}{3}(0.6)$$

$$f(9 + 0.6) \approx 3.1$$

A comparison to a calculator value of 3.0984 reveals that our

approximation is off by about 0.00161.

4.3 INCREASING AND DECREASING INTERVALS AND RELATIVE EXTREMA

This section and the following three sections will present techniques for analyzing functions using calculus. We begin by examining intervals where functions increase and decrease.

Increasing and Decreasing Intervals

A function is increasing when *y*-values increase as *x*-values increase. A function is decreasing when *y*-values decrease as *x*-values increase. Observe that $f(x) = x^2$ decreases when $x < 0$ and increases when $x > 0$:

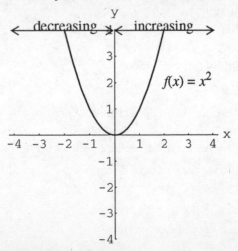

By sketching some tangent lines where $f(x) = x^2$ is decreasing and increasing, we note that the function decreases when the slopes of the tangents are negative, and increases when the slopes of the tangents are positive:

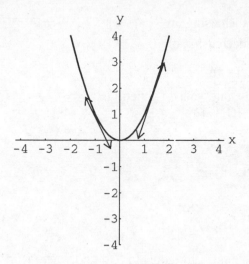

We have the following rules to determine when a differentiable function is increasing or decreasing.

To Determine Intervals Where $f(x)$ is Increasing or Decreasing:

1. Find $f'(x)$.
2. Find critical numbers - that is, where $f'(x) = 0$ or where $f'(x)$ is undefined.
3. Draw a number line, dot in the critical numbers and determine the sign of $f'(x)$ within each region.
4. Where $f'(x) > 0$ (+ on the number line), $f(x)$ is increasing.
5. Where $f'(x) < 0$ (– on the number line), $f(x)$ is decreasing.

EXAMPLE 9

Find the intervals on which $f(x) = x^3 - 4x^2 + 1$ is increasing or decreasing.

SOLUTION 9

$(f')\,(x) = 3x^2 - 8x$	Find $f'(x)$.
$3x^2 - 8x = 0$	Set $f'(x) = 0$.
$x(3x - 8) = 0$	Factor.

$$x = 0 \quad \text{or} \quad 3x - 8 = 0$$
$$x = \frac{8}{3}$$

Solve for critical number.

$$f'(-1) = +11$$
$$f'(1) = -5$$
$$f'(3) = 3$$

$f(x)$ is increasing on $(-\infty, 0)$ and $(\frac{8}{3}, \infty)$.

$f(x)$ is decreasing on $(0, \frac{8}{3})$.

EXAMPLE 10

Find the intervals on which $f(x) = \dfrac{x^2}{x^2 - 4}$ is increasing and decreasing.

SOLUTION 10

$$f'(x) = \frac{(x^2 - 4)(2x) - (x^2)(2x)}{(x^2 - 4)^2}$$

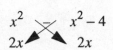

$$f'(x) = \frac{-8x}{(x^2 - 4)^2}$$

Simplify.

Set the numerator equal to 0 to find where $f'(x) = 0$.

$-8x = 0$ Solve for x.

$x = 0$ $x = 0$ is a critical number.

Set the denominator equal to 0 to find where $f'(x)$ is undefined.

$(x^2 - 4)^2 = 0$ Set the denominator = 0.

$x^2 - 4 = 0$ Take the square root of both sides.

$x^2 = 4$ Add 4 to both sides.

$x = \pm 2$ Take the square root of both sides.

Since the denominator is always + when $x \neq \pm 2$, check the sign of $-8x$.

$f(x)$ is increasing on $(-\infty, -2)$ and $(-2, 0)$.

$f(x)$ is decreasing on $(0, 2)$ and $(2, \infty)$.

Extrema

Extrema of a function are the maximum and/or minimum y-values of the function (also called the absolute maximum and absolute minimum).

We will also be interested in finding the relative extrema of a function - that is, the maximum or minimum value within an open interval. The following statements provide reasons for the steps we'll use in finding extrema.

1. A continuous function on a closed interval $[a, b]$ has both a maximum and a minimum.
2. If a function has a relative maximum or relative minimum, it must occur at a critical number.

Extrema on a Closed Interval

If the function $f(x)$ is continuous on a closed interval $[a, b]$, we'll use the following steps to find the absolute maximum and absolute minimum.

Extrema on $[a, b]$

1. Find critical numbers - that is, values of x such that $f'(x) = 0$ or $f'(x)$ is undefined.
2. Evaluate f at each critical number.
3. Evaluate $f(a)$ and $f(b)$.
4. The largest value from steps 2 and 3 is the absolute maximum and the smallest is the absolute minimum.

EXAMPLE 11

Find the absolute maximum and minimum for $f(x) = x^3 - 4x^2 + 1$ on $[-1, 5]$.

SOLUTION 11

We found the critical numbers for $f(x)$ in Example 9 at $x = 0$ and $x = \frac{8}{3}$. We'll proceed to step 2.

$f(0) = 0^3 - 4(0)^2 + 1 = 1$ Evaluate f at each critical number.

$f(\frac{8}{3}) = (\frac{8}{3})^3 - 4(\frac{8}{3})^2 + 1 = -\frac{229}{27} \approx -8.5$

$f(-1) = (-1)^3 - 4(-1)^2 + 1 = -4$ Evaluate f at the endpoints of the interval.

$f(5) = (5)^3 - 4(5)^2 + 1 = 26$

The absolute maximum of 26 occurs when $x = 5$ and the absolute minimum of $-\frac{229}{27}$ occurs when $x = \frac{8}{3}$.

Note from the previous example that an absolute maximum or minimum may occur at either an endpoint of the closed interval *or* at a critical number.

EXAMPLE 12

Find the absolute maximum and minimum for $f(x) = \sin x$ on $[0, \pi]$.

SOLUTION 12

$f'(x) = \cos x$ Find $f'(x)$.

$\cos x = 0$ Set $f'(x) = 0$.

$x = \dfrac{\pi}{2}$ $\dfrac{\pi}{2}$ is a critical number.

$f(\dfrac{\pi}{2}) = \sin \dfrac{\pi}{2} = 1$ Evaluate f at the critical number and each endpoint.

$f(0) = \sin 0 = 0$

$f(\pi) = \sin \pi = 0$

Thus the absolute maximum of 1 occurs at $x = \dfrac{\pi}{2}$ and the absolute minimum of 0 occurs at $x = 0$ and $x = \pi$.

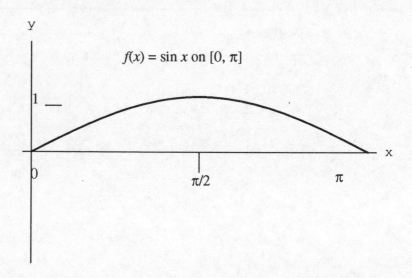

$f(x) = \sin x$ on $[0, \pi]$

Note from this example that maximums and minimums are *y-values*, not *x*-values.

4.4 THE FIRST AND SECOND DERIVATIVE TESTS AND CONCAVITY

Relative Extrema

When a function is *not* defined on a closed interval, we are *not* guaranteed an absolute maximum and minimum. We can, however, find relative extrema using the First Derivative Test. The First Derivative Test states that if the signs of the first derivative change beside a critical number, c, then $f(c)$ is a relative maximum or minimum. The following steps apply when f is a continuous function on an open interval, differentiable except possibly at a critical number.

1. Find $f'(x)$.
2. Find critical numbers - that is, where $f'(c) = 0$ and where $f'(c)$ is undefined.
3. Draw a number line, dot in the critical numbers and determine the sign of $f'(x)$ in each region.
4. Use the following guides to determine whether $f(c)$ is a relative maximum or minimum.

sign of $f'(x)$ $f(c)$ is a relative maximum

$$\underset{c}{+ \mid -}$$

sign of $f'(x)$ $f(c)$ is a relative minimum

$$\underset{c}{- \mid +}$$

sign of $f'(x)$ $f(c)$ is neither a relative maximum or minimum.

$$\underset{c}{- \mid -} \text{ or } \underset{c}{+ \mid +}$$

EXAMPLE 13

Find the relative extrema for $f(x) = x^3 - 4x^2 + 1$

SOLUTION 13

We found the critical numbers for this continuous function in Example 9.

We found the following sign changes for $f'(x)$.

sign of $f'(x)$ $+$ $-$ $+$

                   0 $8/3$

The First Derivative Test tells us that:

$x = 0$ is a relative maximum   Sign change $+$ to $-$.

$x = \dfrac{8}{3}$ is a relative minimum   Sign change $-$ to $+$.

When $x = 0$, $f(0) = 1$, 1 is a relative maximum.

When $x = \frac{8}{3}, f(\frac{8}{3}) = -\frac{229}{27}$ is a relative minimum.

EXAMPLE 14

Find the open intervals on which $f(x) = 3x^4 - x^3 - 24x^2 + 12x$ is increasing or decreasing and find all relative extrema.

SOLUTION 14

$f'(x) = 12x^3 - 3x^2 - 48x + 12$ Find $f'(x)$.

$12x^3 - 3x^2 - 48x + 12 = 0$ Set $f'(x) = 0$ to find critical numbers.

$3x^2(4x - 1) - 12(4x - 1) = 0$

$(4x - 1)(3x^2 - 12) = 0$ Factor by grouping.

$4x - 1 = 0$ or $3x^2 - 12 = 0$ Set each factor equal to 0

$x = \frac{1}{4}$ $x = \pm 2$ and solve.

sign of $f'(x)$ Determine the sign of $f'(x)$ in each region.

$$\begin{array}{ccccc} - & + & - & + \end{array}$$

$$\underset{-2 \qquad 1/4 \quad 2}{\rule{6cm}{0.4pt}}$$

$f(x)$ is increasing on $(-2, \frac{1}{4})$ and $(2, \infty)$.

$f(x)$ is decreasing on $(-\infty, -2)$ and $(\frac{1}{4}, 2)$.

$f(-2) = -64$ is a relative minimum   Sign changes – to +.

$f(\frac{1}{4}) = \frac{383}{256}$ is a relative maximum   Sign changes + to –.

$f(2) = -32$ is a relative minimum   Sign changes – to +.

Concavity

When the graph of a function $f(x)$ lies above its tangent lines, $f(x)$ is concave upward. When the graph of $f(x)$ lies below its tangent lines, $f(x)$ is concave downward. It may also help to think of "holding water" (concave up) or "pouring water" (concave down). Because a function is concave up when $f''(x) > 0$ and concave down when $f''(x) < 0$, we can use the following steps to determine a differentiable function's concavity.

To Find Intervals of Concavity

1. Find $f''(x)$.
2. Find x-values where $f''(x) = 0$ and where $f''(x)$ is undefined.
3. Draw a number line, dot in the values found in step 2 and determine the sign of $f''(x)$ in each region.
4. The function is concave upward where $f''(x) > 0$ and concave downward where $f''(x) < 0$.

EXAMPLE 15

Determine the intervals where $f(x) = x^3 - 4x^2 + 1$ is concave upward and downward.

SOLUTION 15

$f'(x) = 3x^2 - 8x$	Find $f'(x)$.
$f''(x) = 6x - 8$	Find $f''(x)$.
$6x - 8 = 0$	Set $f''(x) = 0$.

$x = \dfrac{8}{6} = \dfrac{4}{3}$ Solve for x.

$$\begin{array}{c} \quad - \;\vdots\; + \\ \overline{\vdots} \\ 4/3 \end{array}$$

sign of $f''(x)$ Dot in $x = \dfrac{4}{3}$. Find the sign of $f''(x)$ in each region.

$f(x)$ is concave downward on $(-\infty, \dfrac{4}{3})$.

$f(x)$ is concave upward on $(\dfrac{4}{3}, \infty)$.

EXAMPLE 16

Determine the intervals where $f(x) = \dfrac{1}{x^2 - 4}$ is concave upward or downward.

SOLUTION 16

$f(x) = (x^2 - 4)^{-1}$ Rewrite $f(x)$.

$f'(x) = -1(x^2 - 4)^{-2}(2x)$ Use the Chain Rule.

$f'(x) = -2x(x^2 - 4)^{-2}$ Simplify.

$$f''(x) = (x^2 - 4)^{-2}(-2) + (-2x)(-4x(x^2-4)^{-3})$$

$$-2x \quad + \quad (x^2-4)^{-2}$$

$$-2 \qquad -2(x^2-4)^{-3}(2x)$$

$$f''(x) = -2(x^2-4)^{-3}[(x^2-4) + x(-4x)] \quad \text{Factor.}$$

$$f''(x) = -2(x^2-4)^{-3}(-3x^2-4) \qquad \text{Simplify.}$$

$$f''(x) = \frac{2(3x^2+4)}{(x^2-4)^3} \qquad \text{Simplify.}$$

$f''(x) = 0$ when the numerator equals 0.

$$2(3x^2+4) = 0 \qquad\qquad \text{Find } f''(x) = 0.$$

$$3x^2 + 4 = 0 \qquad\qquad \text{Solve for } x.$$

$$x^2 = -\frac{4}{3} \qquad\qquad \text{This has no real solutions.}$$

$f''(x)$ is undefined when the denominator equals 0.

$$(x^2-4)^3 = 0 \qquad\qquad \text{Find } f''(x) = 0.$$

$$x^2 - 4 = 0 \qquad\qquad \text{Solve for } x.$$
$$x = \pm 2$$
$$\text{sign of } f''(x) \qquad\qquad \text{Determine the sign of } f''(x)$$
in each region.

$f(x)$ is concave upward on $(-\infty, -2)$ and $(2, \infty)$.

$f(x)$ is concave downward on $(-2, 2)$.

Inflection Points

The point where a function changes from being concave upward to concave downward or vice versa is called an inflection point. The procedure for finding inflection points is the same as the procedure for finding intervals of concavity. Be careful to determine whether the x-values where the concavity changes are in the domain of $f(x)$.

EXAMPLE 17

Find the inflection point, if any, for each function.

a) $f(x) = x^3 - 4x^2 + 1$

b) $f(x) = \dfrac{1}{x^2 - 4}$

SOLUTION 17

a) Returning to Example 15, we know

sign of $f''(x)$

4/3

Thus the concavity changes at $x = \dfrac{4}{3}$. The inflection point is

$(\dfrac{4}{3}, f(\dfrac{4}{3})) = (\dfrac{4}{3}, -\dfrac{101}{27})$.

b) Returning to Example 16, we know

sign of $f''(x)$

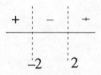

−2   2

However, $x = -2$ and $x = 2$ are *not* x-values for inflection points because the denominator of $f(x) = \dfrac{1}{x^2 - 4}$ does *not* include −2 and

2. There are no inflection points for $f(x)$.

Second Derivative Test

An alternative technique exists for finding relative maximums and minimums. This technique is based on the Second Derivative Test.

> **To Find Relative Extrema Using the Second Derivative Test:**
> 1. Find $f'(x)$.
> 2. Find $f''(x)$.
> 3. Solve $f'(c) = 0$.
> 4. If $f''(c) > 0$, then $f(c)$ is a relative minimum.
>   If $f''(c) < 0$, then $f(c)$ is a relative maximum.
>   If $f''(c) = 0$, return to the First Derivative Test to analyze $f(c)$.

EXAMPLE 18

Use the Second Derivative Test to find the relative extrema for each function.

a) $f(x) = 2x^4 + 3x^3 - 1$

b) $f(x) = \sin x + \cos x$ on $[0, 2\pi]$

c) $f(x) = x^5 - x^4 + 1$

SOLUTION 18

a) $f'(x) = 8x^3 + 9x^2$ Find $f'(x)$.

$f''(x) = 24x^2 + 18x$ Find $f''(x)$.

$8x^3 + 9x^2 = 0$ Set $f'(x) = 0$.

$x^2(8x + 9) = 0$ Factor.

$x = 0$ or $x = -\dfrac{9}{8}$ Solve.

$f''(0) = 24(0)^2 + 18(0) = 0$ Find $f''(0)$.

$f''(-\dfrac{9}{8}) = 24(-\dfrac{9}{8})^2 + 18(-\dfrac{9}{8}) = \dfrac{81}{8}$ Find $f''(-\dfrac{9}{8})$.

Since $f''(0) = 0$, the Second Derivative Test fails.

First Derivative Test:

$$+ \mid + \quad \text{sign of } f'(x)$$
$$0$$

Since there is no sign change, $(0, -1)$ is neither a relative maximum nor a relative minimum. It is, however, an inflection point:

$$- \mid + \quad \text{sign of } f''(x)$$
$$0$$

Since $f''(-\frac{9}{8}) > 0$, $(-\frac{9}{8}, -2.06)$ is a relative minimum.

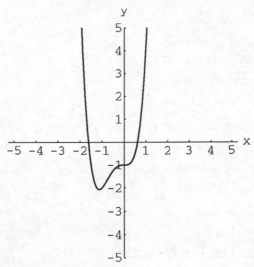

b) $f'(x) = \cos x - \sin x$ Find $f'(x)$.

$f''(x) = -\sin x - \cos x$ Find $f''(x)$.

$\cos x - \sin x = 0$ Set $f'(x) = 0$.

$\cos x = \sin x$ Add $\sin x$ to both sides.

$$\frac{\cos x}{\cos x} = \frac{\sin x}{\cos x} \qquad \text{Divide by } \cos x.$$

$$1 = \tan x \qquad\qquad \text{Use } \frac{\sin x}{\cos x} = \tan x.$$

$$x = \frac{\pi}{4}, \frac{5\pi}{4}$$

$$f''\left(\frac{\pi}{4}\right) = -\sin\frac{\pi}{4} - \cos\frac{\pi}{4} = -\sqrt{2}$$

$$f''\left(\frac{5\pi}{4}\right) = -\sin\frac{5\pi}{4} - \cos\frac{5\pi}{4} = -\left(-\frac{\sqrt{2}}{2}\right) - \left(-\frac{\sqrt{2}}{2}\right) = \sqrt{2}$$

Since $f''\left(\frac{\pi}{4}\right) < 0$, $\left(\frac{\pi}{4}, \sqrt{2}\right)$ is a relative maximum.

Since $f''\left(\frac{5\pi}{4}\right) > 0$, $\left(\frac{5\pi}{4}, -\sqrt{2}\right)$ is a relative minimum.

c) $f(x) = x^5 - x^4 + 1$
$f'(x) = 5x^4 - 4x^3$
$f''(x) = 20x^3 - 12x^2$

$5x^4 - 4x^3 = 0$
$x^3(5x - 4) = 0$
$x = 0 \quad$ or $\quad x = \frac{4}{5}$

$f''(0) = 20\,(0)^3 - 12\,(0)^2 = 0 \qquad$ Test fails.

$$f''\left(\frac{4}{5}\right) = 20\left(\frac{4}{5}\right)^3 - 12\left(\frac{4}{5}\right)^2 = 2\frac{14}{25} \quad f''\left(\frac{4}{5}\right) > 0.$$

We know $\left(\frac{4}{5}, \frac{2869}{3125}\right)$ is a relative maximum. Since $f''(0) = 0$, we use the First Derivative Test:

sign of $f'(x)$

$$+ \ \vdots \ +$$
$$0$$

Since there is no sign change, $(0, 0)$ is neither a relative maximum nor a relative minimum (try testing for an inflection point).

4.5 LIMITS AT INFINITY AND INFINITE LIMITS

Limits at Infinity

The topic of horizontal asymptotes is studied in precalculus courses. We can now examine that topic using limit notation. If a function $f(x)$ approaches a y-value L as x approaches positive infinity, we write

$$\lim_{x \to \infty} f(x) = L$$

We call L a horizontal asymptote of $f(x)$. If a function $f(x)$ approaches a y-value of N as x approaches negative infinity we write

$$\lim_{x \to -\infty} f(x) = N$$

and N is a horizontal asymptote for $f(x)$. We'll use the following procedure to evaluate limits as x approaches positive or negative infinity (and find horizontal asymptotes).

To Evaluate Limits at Infinity

1. Divide each term in the numerator and denominator by the highest power of x in the denominator.

2. Use the fact that the limit of a constant divided by a rational power of x as x approaches infinity equals 0 (and $\lim\limits_{x \to -\infty} \dfrac{c}{x^r} = 0$ provided x^r is defined for $x < 0$ and $r > 0$) to evaluate each limit within the numerator and denominator.

EXAMPLE 19

Find each limit.

a) $\lim\limits_{x \to \infty} \dfrac{4x - 1}{x^2 - 9}$

b) $\lim\limits_{x \to \infty} \dfrac{3x - 1}{2x + 5}$

c) $\lim\limits_{x \to \infty} \dfrac{x^3 + 4x + 1}{x^2 + 2}$

SOLUTION 19

a) $\lim\limits_{x \to \infty} \dfrac{4x-1}{x^2-9} = \lim\limits_{x \to \infty} \dfrac{\dfrac{4x}{x^2}-\dfrac{1}{x^2}}{\dfrac{x^2}{x^2}-\dfrac{9}{x^2}}$ Divide each term by x^2.

$= \lim\limits_{x \to \infty} \dfrac{\dfrac{4}{x}-\dfrac{1}{x^2}}{1-\dfrac{9}{x^2}}$ Simplify.

$= \dfrac{0-0}{1+0}$ Evaluate each limit.

$= \dfrac{0}{1} = 0$

b) $\lim\limits_{x \to \infty} \dfrac{3x-1}{2x+5} = \lim\limits_{x \to \infty} \dfrac{\dfrac{3x}{x}-\dfrac{1}{x}}{\dfrac{2x}{x}+\dfrac{5}{x}}$ Divide each term by x.

$= \lim\limits_{x \to \infty} \dfrac{3-\dfrac{1}{x}}{2+\dfrac{5}{x}}$ Simplify.

$= \dfrac{3-0}{2+0}$ Evaluate each limit.

$= \dfrac{3}{2}$

c) $\lim\limits_{x \to \infty} \dfrac{x^3+4x+1}{x^2+2} = \lim\limits_{x \to \infty} \dfrac{\dfrac{x^3}{x^2}+\dfrac{4x}{x^2}+\dfrac{1}{x^2}}{\dfrac{x^2}{x^2}+\dfrac{2}{x^2}}$ Divide each term by x^2.

$= \lim\limits_{x \to \infty} \dfrac{x+\dfrac{4}{x}+\dfrac{1}{x^2}}{1+\dfrac{2}{x^2}}$ Simplify.

$= \lim\limits_{x \to \infty} \dfrac{x}{1}$ Evaluate each limit.

Since the numerator increases without bound, this limit does not exist.

EXAMPLE 20

Find each limit.

a) $\displaystyle\lim_{x \to -\infty} \frac{3x+5}{x-2}$

b) $\displaystyle\lim_{x \to -\infty} \frac{x^2+6x}{x^3-1}$

SOLUTION 20

a) $\displaystyle\lim_{x \to -\infty} \frac{3x+5}{x-2} = \lim_{x \to -\infty} \frac{\dfrac{3x}{x}+\dfrac{5}{x}}{\dfrac{x}{x}-\dfrac{2}{x}}$ Divide each term by x.

$\displaystyle = \lim_{x \to -\infty} \frac{3+\dfrac{5}{x}}{1-\dfrac{2}{x}}$ Simplify.

$\displaystyle = \frac{3+0}{1-0}$ Evaluate each limit.

$= 3$

b) $\displaystyle\lim_{x \to -\infty} \frac{x^2+6x}{x^3-1} = \lim_{x \to -\infty} \frac{\dfrac{x^2}{x^3}+\dfrac{6x}{x^3}}{\dfrac{x^3}{x^3}-\dfrac{1}{x^3}}$ Divide each term by x^3.

$\displaystyle = \lim_{x \to -\infty} \frac{\dfrac{1}{x}+\dfrac{6}{x^2}}{1-\dfrac{1}{x^3}}$ Simplify.

$\displaystyle = \frac{0+0}{1-0} = \frac{0}{1} = 0$ Evaluate each limit.

Infinite Limits

We use the definition of an infinite limit to help describe when the y-values of a function increase or decrease without bound as the x-values approach some number c. The following list presents the various situations and the associated notation.

$$\lim_{x \to c^+} f(x) = +\infty \qquad \lim_{x \to c^+} f(x) = -\infty \qquad \lim_{x \to c^-} f(x) = +\infty$$

$$\lim_{x \to c^-} f(x) = -\infty \qquad \lim_{x \to c} f(x) = \infty \qquad \lim_{x \to c} f(x) = -\infty$$

These infinite limits occur around vertical asymptotes - that is where the denominator of a function is *not* a factor of the numerator and equals 0. It is generally easiest to use reasoning to find these limits. Study Example 21.

EXAMPLE 21

Find each limit.

a) $\displaystyle \lim_{x \to 1^+} \frac{5}{x - 1}$

b) $\displaystyle \lim_{x \to 1^-} \frac{5}{x - 1}$

c) $\displaystyle \lim_{x \to 2^+} \frac{4x}{(x - 2)^2}$

d) $\displaystyle \lim_{x \to 2^-} \frac{4x}{(x - 2)^2}$

e) $\displaystyle \lim_{x \to 2} \frac{4x}{(x - 2)^2}$

SOLUTION 21

a) We reason in the following manner. As x approaches 1 from the right, $x - 1$ will be positive. The numerator is always positive. Thus

$$\lim_{x \to 1^+} \frac{5}{x-1} = +\infty.$$

b) As x approaches 1 from the left, $x - 1$ will be negative. The numerator is always positive. Thus

$$\lim_{x \to 1^-} \frac{5}{x-1} = -\infty.$$

c) & d) As x approaches 2 from the left or right, $(x-2)^2$ will always be positive. The numerator will be positive when x approaches 2 from the left or right. Thus

$$\lim_{x \to 2^+} \frac{4x}{(x-2)^2} = \lim_{x \to 2^-} \frac{4x}{(x-2)^2} = +\infty.$$

e) Since the limit from the left and the limit from the right both equal $+\infty$, we write

$$\lim_{x \to 2} \frac{4x}{(x-2)^2} = +\infty.$$

4.6 GRAPHING USING THE TOOLS OF CALCULUS

We can now put all our techniques for analyzing graphs of functions together to draw a sophisticated graph.

Graphing Using Calculus

We can summarize the various graphing aids which can be used to sketch a function. This list is not meant to be memorized, but to act as a guide to help you prepare a sophisticated graph of a function.

1. Find the domain of $f(x)$.
2. Find the x-intercept(s) and the y-intercept.
3. Check for symmetry with respect to the y-axis and origin.
4. Dot in horizontal and vertical asymptotes.
5. Find relative extrema.
6. Find intervals where $f(x)$ is increasing and decreasing (use the first derivative) and where $f(x)$ is concave upward and downward (use the second derivative).
7. Note any points of inflection.

EXAMPLE 22

Sketch the graph of $f(x) = (x-1)^2(x+2)$.

SOLUTION 22

1. The domain is all real numbers since this is a polynomial function.

2. If $y = 0$, $(x-1)^2(x+2) = 0$ means $x = 1$ or $x = -2$.

    If $x = 0$, $f(0) = (0-1)^2(0+2) = 2$.

    The x-intercepts are 1 and -2.

    The y-intercept is 2.

3. Replacing x with $-x$ does not yield an equivalent equation so $f(x)$ is not symmetric with respect to the y-axis. Replacing x with $-x$ and y with $-y$ does not yield an equivalent equation so $f(x)$ is not symmetric with respect to the origin.

4. No asymptotes.

5. $f'(x) = (x+2)(2)(x-1) + (x-1)^2$ $(x-1)^2$  $(x+2)$

    $f'(x) = (x-1)(2x+4+x-1)$ $2(x-1)$ 1

    $f'(x) = (x-1)(3x+3)$

    $f'(x) = 0$ when $x = 1$ and $x = -1$.

    We'll find increasing and decreasing intervals and relative extrema with the first derivative:

    sign of $f'(x)$

    $$+ \quad\quad - \quad\quad +$$
    $$\underline{\qquad\qquad\qquad\qquad\qquad}$$
    $$\quad -1 \quad\quad 1$$

    $f(x)$ is increasing on $(-\infty, -1)$ and $(1, \infty)$.

    $f(x)$ is decreasing on $(-1, 1)$.

    $(-1, f(-1)) = (-1, 4)$ is a relative maximum.

    $(1, f(1)) = (1, 0)$ is a relative minimum.

6. It's easier to multiply out $f'(x)$ before finding $f''(x)$.

    $f'(x) = (x-1)(3x+3) = 3x^2 - 3$

    $f''(x) = 6x$

    $f''(x) = 0$ when $x = 0$

sign of $f''(x)$

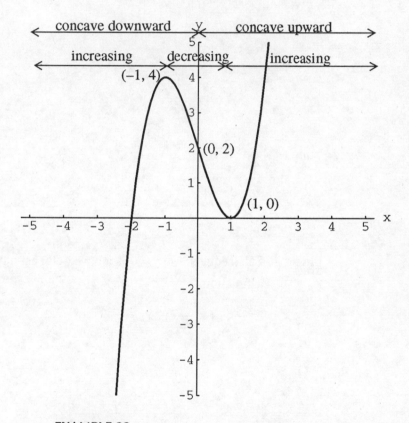

$f(x)$ is concave downward on $(-\infty, 0)$.

$f(x)$ is concave upward on $(0, -\infty)$.

7. $(0, f(0)) = (0, 2)$ is an inflection point.

Putting all this information together we have:

EXAMPLE 23

Sketch the graph of $f(x) = \dfrac{x}{x^2 - 4}$.

SOLUTION 23

1. To find the domain, set the denominator equal to 0 to find restricted values.

$$x^2 - 4 = 0$$

$$x^2 = 4$$

$x = \pm 2$

The domain is all real numbers *except* –2 and 2.

2. If $y = 0$, $x = 0$.

   If $x = 0$, $y = 0$.

   (0, 0) is the x-intercept and y-intercept.

3. Replacing x with $-x$ and y with $-y$ yields an equivalent equation, so $f(x)$ is symmetric with respect to the origin.

4. There are vertical asymptotes at $x = 2$ and $x = -2$.

   To find horizontal asymptotes, check the limit of $f(x)$ as x approaches positive and negative infinity.

   $$\lim_{x \to \infty} \frac{x}{x^2 - 4} = \lim_{x \to \infty} \frac{\dfrac{x}{x^2}}{\dfrac{x^2}{x^2} - \dfrac{4}{x^2}}$$

   $$= \lim_{x \to \infty} \frac{\dfrac{1}{x}}{1 - \dfrac{4}{x^2}}$$

   $$= \frac{0}{1 - 0} = 0$$

   $\lim_{x \to -\infty} \dfrac{x}{x^2 - 4}$ also equals 0 so $y = 0$ is a horizontal asymptote for the function.

5. $f'(x) = \dfrac{(x^2 - 4)(1) - x(2x)}{(x^2 - 4)^2}$

   $$\begin{array}{ccc} x & \diagdown & x^2 - 4 \\ 1 & \diagup & 2x \end{array}$$

   $$f'(x) = \frac{-x^2 - 4}{(x^2 - 4)^2}$$

   The only critical numbers occur when the denominator equals 0 since $-x^2 - 4$ can never equal 0.

   If $x^2 - 4 = 0$ $x = \pm 2$

sign of $f'(x)$

-2   0   2

$f(x)$ is decreasing on $(-\infty, -2)$, $(-2, -2)$, and $(2, \infty)$.

There are no maximums or minimums since the sign changes in the first derivative occurred around values that are *not* in the domain of $f(x)$.

6. $-x^2 - 4 \quad (x^2 - 4)^2$
    $-2x \qquad 4x(x^2 - 4)$

    Use the Quotient Rule to find $f''(x)$.

    $$f''(x) = \frac{(x^2 - 4)^2(-2x) - (-x^2 - 4)(4x)(x^2 - 4)}{(x^2 - 4)^4}$$

    $$f''(x) = \frac{-2x(x^2 - 4)[(x^2 - 4) + (-x^2 - 4)(2)]}{(x^2 - 4)^4}$$

    Factor.

    $$f''(x) = \frac{-2x(x^2 - 4)(-x^2 - 12)}{(x^2 - 4)^4}$$

    Simplify.

    $$f''(x) = \frac{2x(x^2 + 12)}{(x^2 - 4)^3}$$

    Reduce.

    $f''(x) = 0$ when $2x(x^2 + 12) = 0$, which is only true when $x = 0$ since $x^2 + 12$ cannot equal 0. $f''(x)$ is undefined when $(x^2 - 4) = 0$, which is when $x = \pm 2$.

    sign of $f''(x)$

    $f(x)$ is concave upward on $(-2, 0)$ and $(2, \infty)$.

    $f(x)$ is concave downward on $(-\infty, -2)$ and $(0, 2)$.

7. Since the sign of $f''(x)$ changes when $x = 0$, $(0, 0)$ is an inflection point. Note that $x = -2$ and $x = 2$ cannot be x-coordinates of inflection points since they are not in the domain of $f(x)$.

Putting all this information together we have the following graph:

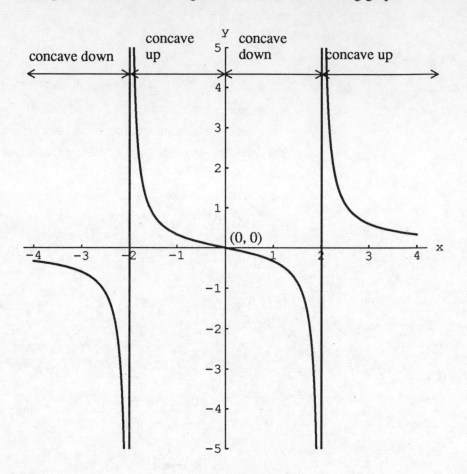

4.7 APPLICATIONS INVOLVING MAXI-MUMS AND MINIMUMS

Applications involving maximums and minimums generally contain information to form two equations. One of these equations will be the function whose maximum or minimum we seek. The other equation should relate the variables in such a way that we can solve it for x or y. A general procedure is outlined below.

Solving Max-Min Applications

1. Draw and label a sketch, as necessary. Identify what each variable represents.
2. Write an equation that represents what is to be maximized or minimized. This equation will be in the form $F =$ _ _ _ _ _ where F is the name you choose for your function.
3. Write an equation that relates the variables from F. Solve this equation for x or y.
4. Substitute for x or y in F.
5. Find maximums or minimums by finding F', then critical numbers, and using the First or Second Derivative Tests.
6. Answer the original question, using appropriate units of measurement (feet, inches, etc.).

EXAMPLE 24

Find two positive numbers whose sum is 56 and whose product is a maximum.

SOLUTION 24

Let $x =$ one number $y =$ other number	Identify what each variable represents.
$P = xy$	Let P represent product.
$x + y = 56$	Write an equation that relates x and y.
$y = 56 - x$	Solve for y.
$P = x(56 - x)$	Substitute into P.
$P = 56x - x^2$	Simplify.
$P' = 56 - 2x$	Find P'.
$56 - 2x = 0$	Find critical numbers.
$x = 28$	

$P'' = -2$ which means $x = 28$ is a maximum.

(Second derivative < 0 implies maximum)

If $x = 28$, $y = 56 - x = 56 - 28 = 28$.

The two numbers are 28 and 28.	Answer the original question.

EXAMPLE 25

A farmer wishes to enclose two identical adjacent rectangular areas, each with 400 square feet of area. What dimensions should be used to minimize the amount of fencing required?

SOLUTION 25

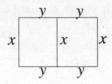

Draw a sketch and label the sides.

Then we know

$$xy = 400$$

Enclosed area of each is 400 sq. ft.

$$F = 3x + 4y$$

Let F equal the amount of fencing.

$$F = 3x + 4\left(\frac{400}{x}\right)$$

$$xy = 400 \Rightarrow y = \frac{400}{x}$$

$$F = 3x + 1600x^{-1}$$

Simplify F.

$$F' = 3 - 1600x^{-2}$$

Find F'.

$$F' = \frac{3x^2 - 1600}{x^2}$$

$x^{-2} = \frac{1}{x^2}$. Get a common denominator.

Find critical numbers:

$$3x^2 - 1600 = 0$$

Set the numerator equal to 0.

$$x = \pm\sqrt{\frac{1600}{3}}$$

$$x = \pm\frac{40}{\sqrt{3}}$$

$$x^2 = 0$$

Set the denominator equal to 0.

$$x = 0$$

Neither 0 nor $-\dfrac{40}{\sqrt{3}}$ can be the answer since neither makes sense for the

length of a side. Let's check $x = \dfrac{40}{\sqrt{3}}$ in the second derivative test:

$$F'' = \frac{x^2(6x) - (3x^2 - 1600)(2x)}{x^4} \qquad \text{Use the Quotient Rule.}$$

$$F'' = \frac{6x^3 - 6x^3 + 3200x}{x^4} \qquad \text{Simplify.}$$

$$F'' = \frac{3200}{x^3} \qquad \text{Reduce.}$$

$$F''\left(\frac{40}{\sqrt{3}}\right) > 0 \Rightarrow x = \frac{40}{\sqrt{3}} \text{ is minimum.}$$

When $x = \dfrac{40}{\sqrt{3}}, y = \dfrac{400}{\dfrac{40}{\sqrt{3}}} = 10\sqrt{3}$.

The dimensions are $\dfrac{40}{\sqrt{3}}$ feet by $10\sqrt{3}$ feet or approximately 23 feet by 17 feet.

*T*his *chapter contained three important applications of derivatives - related rates, graphing, and maximum-minimum word problems. We found maximums and minimums using the First Derivative Test (find critical numbers, test for sign changes on either side of them) and the Second Derivative Test (find critical numbers, substitute them into the second derivative, if f''(c) > 0, c is a minimum and if f''(c) < 0, c is a maximum). The following chapters focus on integration and we shall find that our skills with derivatives are essential to success with integration.*

Practice Exercises

1. Use implicit differentiation to find the derivative with respect to time.

(a) $A = \dfrac{\sqrt{3}}{4}s^2$

(b) $V = \dfrac{4}{3}\pi r^3$

(c) $S = 4\pi r^2$

2. Oil spills into a lake in a circular pattern. If the radius of the circle increases at a rate of 6 inches per minute, how fast is the area of the spill increasing at the end of 1 hour? Give your answer in ft²/min.

3. Air is being pumped into a spherical balloon at a rate of 4 cubic inches per minute. Find the rate of change of the radius when the radius is 8 inches.

4. A 10 foot ladder is leaning against the wall of a house. The base of the ladder slides away from the wall at a rate of 3 inches per second. How fast is the top of the ladder moving down the wall when the base is 5 feet from the wall?

5. A weather balloon is releases 20 feet from an observer. It rises at a rate of 4 feet per second. How fast is the angle of elevation changing when the balloon is 20 feet high?

6. Find the differential, dy, for each function.

(a) $y = 2x^4 - 3x^2 + 4$

(b) $y = (x^2 + 6x)^4$

(c) $y = x\cos 2x$

7. Use differentials to approximate

(a) $\sqrt{4.2}$

(b) $\sqrt{3.8}$

8. Find the intervals on which the function is increasing and decreasing.

(a) $f(x) = x^4 - 2x^2 + 1$

(b) $f(x) = \dfrac{2x^2}{4x^2 - 1}$

9. Find the absolute maximum and minimumon the indicated closed interval.

(a) $f(x) = x^2 + 2x - 1$ on [–2,2]

(b) $f(x) = 2\cos x$ on [0, 3π/2]

10. Find the relative extrema for each function.

(a) $f(x) = \dfrac{1}{3}x^3 + x^2 - 3x + 2$

(b) $f(x) = \dfrac{x - 3}{2x + 1}$

(c) $f(x) = \dfrac{1}{4}x^4 - x^3 - \dfrac{1}{2}x^2 + 3x$

11. Determine the intervals where the function is concave upward or concave downward.

(a) $f(x) = \dfrac{1}{12}x^4 - \dfrac{1}{2}x^3 - 5x^2$

(b) $f(x) = \dfrac{4x}{x-2}$

12. Find the inflection point(s), if any, for each function.

(a) $f(x) = \dfrac{1}{12}x^4 - \dfrac{1}{2}x^3 - 5x^2$

(b) $f(x) = \dfrac{4x}{x-2}$

13. Use the Second Derivative Test to find the relative extrema for each function.

(a) $f(x) = \dfrac{1}{3}x^3 - 2x^2 - 5x$

(b) $f(x) = \sqrt{3}\sin x + \cos x$ on $[0, 2\pi]$

14. Find each limit.

(a) $\lim\limits_{x \to \infty} \dfrac{x+4}{x^2-1}$

(b) $\lim\limits_{x \to \infty} \dfrac{6x+1}{2x-5}$

(c) $\lim\limits_{x \to \infty} \dfrac{2x^2-4x+1}{x-3}$

15. Find each limit.

(a) $\lim\limits_{x \to -\infty} \dfrac{2x-1}{x+4}$

(b) $\lim\limits_{x \to -\infty} \dfrac{x^3-2x^2+4x+2}{x^2-1}$

16. Find each limit.

(a) $\lim\limits_{x \to 2^+} \dfrac{x}{x-2}$

(b) $\lim\limits_{x \to 2^-} \dfrac{x}{x-2}$

(c) $\lim\limits_{x \to -1^+} \dfrac{x-4}{(x+1)^2}$

(d) $\lim\limits_{x \to -1^-} \dfrac{x-4}{(x+1)^2}$

17. Use all the graphing skills developed to sketch each graph. Note the relative extrema, inflection points, asymptotes, increasing and decreasing intervals and concave upward and downward intervals.

(a) $f(x) = \dfrac{1}{4}x^4 - x^3 - 2x^2$

(b) $f(x) = \dfrac{x^2+1}{x^2-4}$

18. Find two positive numbers whose sum is 108 and whose product is a maximum.

19. A farmer wishes to enclose three identical adjacent rectangular areas, each with 900 square feet of area. What dimensions should be used to minimize the amount of fence required?

Answers

1.

(a) $\dfrac{dA}{dt} = \dfrac{\sqrt{3}}{2} s \dfrac{ds}{dt}$

(b) $\dfrac{dV}{dt} = 4\pi r^2 \dfrac{dr}{dt}$

(c) $\dfrac{dS}{dt} = 8\pi r \dfrac{dr}{dt}$

2. 30π ft²/min

3. $\dfrac{1}{64\pi}$ in/min

4. $(-\sqrt{3})$ in/sec

5.   0.1 rad/sec

6.

(a) $(8x^3 - 6x)\,dx$

(b) $8(x+3)(x^2 + 6x)^3\,dx$

(c) $(\cos 2x - 2x \sin 2x)\,dx$

7.

(a)   2.05

(b)   1.95

8.

(a)   increasing $(-1, 0)$ and $(1, \infty)$

decreasing $(-\infty, -1)$ and $(0, 1)$

(b)   increasing $(-\infty, -1/2)$ and $(-1/2, 0)$

decreasing $(0, 1/2)$ and $(1/2, \infty)$

9.

(a)   absolute maximum $(2, 7)$

absolute minimum $(-1, -2)$

(b)   absolute maximum $(0, 2)$

absolute minimum $(\pi, -2)$

10.

(a)   relative maximum $(-3, 11)$

relative minimum $(1, 1/3)$

(b)   no relative extrema

(c)   relative maximum $(1, 7/4)$

relative minimum $(-1, -9/4)$ and $(3, -9/4)$

11.

(a)   concave upward $(-\infty, -2)$ $(5, \infty)$

concave downward $(-2, 5)$

(b)   concave upward $(2, \infty)$

concave downward $(-\infty, 2)$

12.

(a) $(-2, -14\frac{2}{3})$ $(5, -135\frac{5}{12})$

(b)   no inflection points

13.

(a)   relative maximum $(-1, 8/3)$

relative minimum $(5, -33\frac{1}{3})$

(b)   relative maximum $(\pi/3, 2)$

relative minimum $(4\pi/3, -2)$

14.

(a)   0

(b)   3

(c)   does not exist

15.

(a)   2

(b)   does not exist

16.

(a) $+\infty$

(b) $-\infty$

(c) $-\infty$

(d) $-\infty$

17.(a)

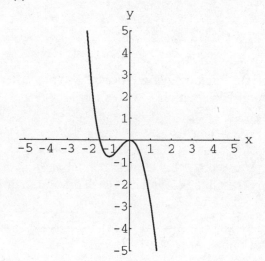

(b)

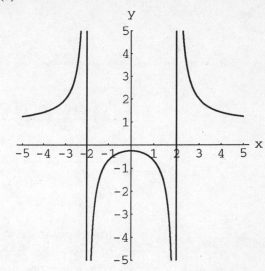

18.   54

19.   Each pen should be $10\sqrt{6}$ feet by $15\sqrt{6}$ feet or approximately 24.5 feet by 36.7 feet.

5

Integrals

In this chapter we will reverse the process of differentiation. Then we will use this new process to find areas bounded by functions and the x-axis. Because this process will require differentiation, you may need to review parts of Chapter 3 as you work through Chapter 5.

5.1 ANTIDERIVATIVES

Just as multiplication and factoring are reverse processes, so are differentiation and antidifferentiation. The notation

$$\int f(x)\, dx$$

is read "the integral of $f(x)$". You need both the integral symbol, $\int$, and dx to imply integration. Study the table below that relates differentiation and integration.

Function	Derivative	Integral
$f(x) = \frac{1}{2}x^2$	$D_x\left[\frac{1}{2}x^2\right] = x$	$\int x\, dx = \frac{1}{2}x^2 + c$
$f(x) = \sin x$	$D_x[\sin x] = \cos x$	$\int \cos x\, dx = \sin x + c$
$f(x) = \frac{1}{3}x^3$	$D_x\left[\frac{1}{3}x^3\right] = x^2$	$\int x^2\, dx = \frac{1}{3}x^3 + c$

Note that $D_x \left[\frac{1}{2}x^2 + 6 \right] = D_x \left[\frac{1}{2}x^2 + 4 \right] = D_x \left[\frac{1}{2}x^2 + c \right]$ for c a con-

stant because the derivative of a constant is 0. Thus, when we integrate x, we write $+ c$ (plus a constant) to account for any constant that may have been present in the original function.

Just as we had formulas for finding derivatives, we have formulas for reversing the process to find integrals. There are books filled with integration formulas. We shall concentrate on the following few. You must memorize this list.

Integration formulas

$\int 0 dx = 0 + c = c$ The integral of 0 is a constant.

$\int k dx = kx + c$ The integral of a constant is the constant times
x plus a constant.

$\int k f(x) \, dx = k \int f(x) \, dx$
The integral of a constant times a function is
the constant times the integral of the function.

$\int [f(x) \pm g(x)] \, dx = \int f(x) \, dx \pm \int g(x) \, dx$
The integral of a sum or difference is the sum
or difference of the integrals.

$\int u^n du = \frac{u^{n+1}}{n+1} + c, n \neq -1$ Power Rule

$\int \cos u \, du = \sin u + c$

$\int \sin u \, du = -\cos u + c$

$\int \sec^2 u \, du = \tan u + c$

EXAMPLE 1

Find each integral.

a) $\int 6 dx$

b) $\int x^6 dx$

c) $\int (x^3 + x^2)\, dx$

d) $\int 5x^{-2} dx$

SOLUTION 1

a) $\int 6dx = 6x + c$

The integral of a constant is the constant times x plus a constant.

b) $\int x^6 dx = \dfrac{x^{6+1}}{6+1} + c$

Use the Power Rule. Add 1 to the original exponent and divide by that sum.

$\quad = \dfrac{x^7}{7} + c$

c) $\int (x^3 + x^2)\, dx = \int x^3 dx + \int x^2 dx$

The integral of a sum is the sum of the integrals.

$\quad = \dfrac{x^{3+1}}{3+1} + c_1 + \dfrac{x^{2+1}}{2+1} + c_2$

Use the Power Rule for each term.

$\quad = \dfrac{x^4}{4} + \dfrac{x^3}{3} + (c_1 + c_2)$

Simplify.

$\quad = \dfrac{x^4}{4} + \dfrac{x^3}{3} + c$

The sum of two constants is written as another constant.

d) $\int 5x^{-2} dx = 5\int x^{-2} dx$

Factor out the constant.

$\quad = 5\left[\dfrac{x^{-2+1}}{-2+1}\right] + c$

Use the Power Rule.

$\quad = 5\left[\dfrac{x^{-1}}{-1}\right] + c$

Simplify.

$\quad = -\dfrac{5}{x} + c$

Rewrite $x^{-1} = \dfrac{1}{x}$.

Note from Example 1c that we write a sum of constants as one constant.

Rewriting To Use The Power Rule

The Power Rule is designed to integrate $[\text{function}]^{\text{power}}$. If the given function is not in that form, use exponent laws and/or algebra techniques to rewrite the function before attempting to integrate.

EXAMPLE 2

Integrate.

a) $\displaystyle\int \frac{1}{x^3}\,dx$

b) $\displaystyle\int \sqrt{x}\,dx$

c) $\displaystyle\int \frac{x^3 + x^4}{x^2}\,dx$

d) $\displaystyle\int \sqrt{x}\,(x^2 + \sqrt{x})\,dx$

SOLUTION 2

a) $\displaystyle\int \frac{1}{x^3}\,dx = \int x^{-3}\,dx$ Use exponent laws to rewrite $\dfrac{1}{x^3} = x^{-3}$.

$\displaystyle = \frac{x^{-3+1}}{-3+1} + c$ Use the Power Rule.

$\displaystyle = \frac{x^{-2}}{-2} + c$ Simplify.

$\displaystyle = -\frac{1}{2x^2} + c$ $x^{-2} = \dfrac{1}{x^2}$.

b) $\displaystyle\int \sqrt{x}\,dx = \int x^{1/2}\,dx$ Use exponent laws to rewrite $\sqrt{x} = x^{1/2}$.

$\displaystyle = \frac{x^{\frac{1}{2}+1}}{\frac{1}{2}+1} + c$ Use the Power Rule.

$\displaystyle = \frac{x^{3/2}}{\frac{3}{2}} + c$ Simplify.

$$= \frac{2}{3}x^{3/2} + c \qquad\qquad \frac{1}{\dfrac{3}{2}} = 1 \div \frac{3}{2} = 1 \cdot \frac{2}{3} = \frac{2}{3}.$$

c) $\displaystyle\int \frac{x^3 + x^4}{x^2}\, dx = \int \left(\frac{x^3}{x^2} + \frac{x^4}{x^2}\right) dx$ 　　Use $\dfrac{a+b}{c} = \dfrac{a}{c} + \dfrac{b}{c}$.

$$= \int (x^1 + x^2)\, dx \qquad\qquad \frac{x^m}{x^n} = x^{m-n}$$

$$= \int x^1 dx + \int x^2 dx \qquad\qquad \text{The integral of a sum is the sum of the integrals.}$$

$$= \frac{x^{1+1}}{1+1} + \frac{x^{2+1}}{2+1} + c \qquad\qquad \text{Use the Power Rule.}$$

$$= \frac{x^2}{2} + \frac{x^3}{3} + c \qquad\qquad \text{Simplify.}$$

d) $\displaystyle\int \sqrt{x}\,(x^2 + \sqrt{x})\, dx = \int x^{1/2}\,(x^2 + x^{1/2})\, dx$ Rewrite radicals using fractional exponents.

$$= \int \left(x^{\frac{1}{2}+2} + x^{\frac{1}{2}+\frac{1}{2}}\right) dx \qquad\qquad \text{Use } x^m \cdot x^n = x^{m+n}.$$

$$= \int (x^{5/2} + x^1)\, dx \qquad\qquad \text{Simplify.}$$

$$= \int x^{5/2}\, dx + \int x^1 dx \qquad\qquad \text{The integral of a sum is the sum of the integrals.}$$

$$= \frac{x^{\frac{5}{2}+\frac{2}{2}}}{\dfrac{5}{2}+\dfrac{2}{2}} + \frac{x^{1+1}}{1+1} + c \qquad\qquad \text{Use the Power Rule.}$$

$$= \frac{x^{7/2}}{\dfrac{7}{2}} + \frac{x^2}{2} + c \qquad\qquad \text{Simplify.}$$

$$= \frac{2}{7}x^{7/2} + \frac{1}{2}x^2 + c \qquad\qquad \frac{1}{\dfrac{7}{2}} = 1 \div \frac{7}{2} = 1 \cdot \frac{2}{7} = \frac{2}{7}.$$

Integrating Trigonometric Functions

At this point we have integration formulas for $\sin u$, $\cos u$, and $\sec^2 u$. If other trigonometric functions occur, we may use identities to rewrite them in a form we can integrate. You may wish to review Chapter 2 section 3.

EXAMPLE 3

Integrate.

a) $\displaystyle\int 4\sin x\,dx$

b) $\displaystyle\int (2\sin x + 3\cos x)\,dx$

c) $\displaystyle\int \frac{1 + \cos x \csc x}{\csc x}\,dx$

d) $\displaystyle\int (4x^3 - \sec^2 x)\,dx$

SOLUTION 3

a) $\displaystyle\int 4\sin x\,dx = 4\int \sin x\,dx$ Factor out the constant, 4.

$\quad = 4\,[-\cos x + c_1]$ $\displaystyle\int \sin x\,dx = -\cos x + c$

$\quad = -4\cos x + 4c_1$ Distribute.

$\quad = -4\cos x + c$ 4 times a constant is some other constant so we just write $+\,c$ in our answer.

b) $\displaystyle\int (2\sin x + 3\cos x)\,dx = \int 2\sin x\,dx + \int 3\cos x\,dx$

     The integral of a sum is the sum of the integrals.

$\quad = 2\int \sin x\,dx + 3\int \cos x\,dx$ Factor out the constants.

$\quad = 2\,[-\cos x] + 3\,[\sin x] + c$ Integrate. Combine all constants and write as c.

$$= -2\cos x + 3\sin x + c \qquad \text{Simplify.}$$

c) $\displaystyle\int \frac{1 + \cos x \csc x}{\csc x}\,dx = \int \left(\frac{1}{\csc x} + \frac{\cos x \csc x}{\csc x}\right) dx$

$$\text{Use } \frac{a+b}{c} = \frac{a}{c} + \frac{b}{c}.$$

$$= \int (\sin x + \cos x)\,dx \qquad \text{Use identities to simplify.}$$

$$= -\cos x + \sin x + c \qquad \text{Integrate each term.}$$

d) $\displaystyle\int (4x^3 - \sec^2 x)\,dx = \int (4x^3\,dx) - \int \sec^2 x\,dx$

The integral of a difference is the difference of the integrals.

$$= 4\int x^3\,dx - \int \sec^2 x\,dx \qquad \text{Factor out the constant.}$$

$$= 4\left[\frac{x^{3+1}}{3+1}\right] - [\tan x] + c \qquad \text{Use the Power Rule for } x^3, \text{ and use } \int \sec^2 x\,dx = \tan x.$$

$$= 4\frac{x^4}{4} - \tan x + c \qquad \text{Simplify.}$$

$$= x^4 - \tan x + c \qquad \text{Reduce.}$$

5.2 SIGMA NOTATION

Sigma notation will be used to develop integration as area under a curve. In this section, we will examine the notation, basic properties, and limits involved in sums.

Definition and Notation

The symbol $\sum$ is used as a shorthand notation for addition.

$$\sum_{i=1}^{n} a_i = a_1 + a_2 + a_3 + \dots + a_n$$

The notation at the bottom of the symbol (here "$i = 1$") means to replace i with consecutive integers starting at 1, and ending with the number on the top of the symbol (here n). Then add up the terms.

EXAMPLE 4

Expand each expression.

a) $\displaystyle\sum_{i=1}^{4} i^2$

b) $\displaystyle\sum_{j=2}^{5} (j + 6)$

c) $\displaystyle\sum_{i=1}^{3} \frac{1}{n}(2i + 3)$

SOLUTION 4

a) $\displaystyle\sum_{i=1}^{4} i^2 = (1)^2 + (2)^2 + (3)^2 + (4)^2$

b) $\displaystyle\sum_{j=2}^{5} (j + 6) = (2 + 6) + (3 + 6) + (4 + 6) + (5 + 6)$

c) $\displaystyle\sum_{i=1}^{3} \frac{1}{n}(2i + 3) = \frac{1}{n}(2(1) + 3) + \frac{1}{n}(2(2) + 3) + \frac{1}{n}(2(3) + 3)$

Note that when the index is i, we only replace i with integers. Thus, n remains n in Example 4c.

Properties and Formulas

We will use the following summation properties and formulas:

$$\sum_{i=1}^{n} ka_i = k \sum_{i=1}^{n} a_i$$

A constant, k, can be factored out of a summation.

$$\sum_{i=1}^{n} (a_i \pm b_i) = \sum_{i=1}^{n} a_i \pm \sum_{i=1}^{n} b_i$$

The summation of a sum or difference is the sum or difference of the summations.

$$\sum_{i=1}^{n} c = cn$$

The sum of a constant, c, is c times n. (Note: index must start at 1 to use this formula.)

$$\sum_{i=1}^{n} i = \frac{n(n+1)}{2}$$

Formula for summing consecutive integers.

$$\sum_{i=1}^{n} i^2 = \frac{n(n+1)(2n+1)}{6}$$

Formula for summing squares of consecutive integers.

EXAMPLE 5

Find each sum.

a) $\displaystyle\sum_{i=1}^{5} 2i$

b) $\displaystyle\sum_{i=1}^{100} (4i+6)$

c) $\displaystyle\sum_{i=1}^{100} \frac{i^2}{2}$

SOLUTION 5

a) $\displaystyle\sum_{i=1}^{5} 2i = 2 \sum_{i=1}^{5} i$

Factor out the constant, 2.

$$= 2(1+2+3+4+5)$$

Write out the sum replacing i with integers from 1 to 5.

$$= 2(15) = 30 \qquad \text{Add.}$$

or

$$2 \sum_{i=1}^{5} i = 2 \left(\frac{5(5+1)}{2} \right) \qquad \text{Use } \sum_{i=1}^{n} i = \frac{n(n+1)}{2}.$$

$$= 2 \left(\frac{30}{2} \right) = 30 \qquad \text{Simplify.}$$

b) $\displaystyle \sum_{i=1}^{100} (4i+6) = \sum_{i=1}^{100} 4i + \sum_{i=1}^{100} 6 \qquad$ Use $\displaystyle \sum (a_i + b_i) = \sum a_i + \sum b_i.$

$$= 4 \sum_{i=1}^{100} i + \sum_{i=1}^{100} 6 \qquad \text{Factor out the constant, 4.}$$

$$= 4 \left[\frac{100(100+1)}{2} \right] + 100(6) \qquad \sum_{i=1}^{n} c = nc \text{ for } n = 100, \quad c = 6.$$

$$= 4 \left[\frac{100(101)}{2} \right] + 600 \qquad \text{Simplify.}$$

$$= 4(50)(101) + 600 \qquad \text{Simplify.}$$

$$= 20{,}800 \qquad \text{Multiply, then add.}$$

c) $\displaystyle \sum_{i=1}^{100} \frac{i^2}{2} = \sum_{i=1}^{100} \frac{1}{2} i^2 \qquad$ Rewrite $\dfrac{i^2}{2} = \dfrac{1}{2} i^2.$

$$= \frac{1}{2} \sum_{i=1}^{100} i^2 \qquad \text{Factor out the constant, } \frac{1}{2}$$

$$= \frac{1}{2} \left[\frac{100(100+1)(2(100)+1)}{6} \right] \qquad \text{Use the formula for } \sum i^2.$$

$$= \frac{1}{2} \left[\frac{100(101)(201)}{6} \right] = 169{,}175$$

Finding Infinite Limits of Sums

Recall from section 4.5 that we can find a limit as x approaches infinity by dividing by the highest power of x in the denominator and using

$$\lim_{x \to \infty} \frac{k}{x^n} = 0, k \text{ a constant.} \text{ We'll use that process to find infinite limits of}$$

summations.

EXAMPLE 6

Find each limit.

a) $\displaystyle \lim_{n \to \infty} \sum_{i=1}^{n} \frac{2i}{n^2}$

b) $\displaystyle \lim_{n \to \infty} \sum_{i=1}^{n} \frac{i^2}{n^3}$

SOLUTION 6

a) $\displaystyle \lim_{n \to \infty} \sum_{i=1}^{n} \frac{2i}{n^2} = \lim_{n \to \infty} \frac{2}{n^2} \sum_{i=1}^{n} i$ Factor out the constant, $\dfrac{2}{n^2}$.

$\displaystyle = \lim_{n \to \infty} \frac{2}{n^2} \left[\frac{n(n+1)}{2} \right]$ Use $\displaystyle \sum_{i=1}^{n} i = \frac{n(n+1)}{2}$.

$\displaystyle = \lim_{n \to \infty} \frac{n+1}{n}$ Reduce $\dfrac{2n}{n^2 \cdot 2} = \dfrac{1}{n}$.

$\displaystyle = \lim_{n \to \infty} \frac{\frac{n}{n} + \frac{1}{n}}{\frac{n}{n}}$ Divide each term by n^1.

$\displaystyle = \lim_{n \to \infty} \frac{1 + \frac{1}{n}}{1}$ Reduce.

$\displaystyle = \frac{1+0}{1} = 1$ Use $\displaystyle \lim_{n \to \infty} \frac{1}{n} = 0$.

b) $\displaystyle\lim_{n \to \infty} \sum_{i=1}^{n} \frac{i^2}{n^3} = \lim_{n \to \infty} \frac{1}{n^3} \sum_{i=1}^{n} i^2$ Factor out the constant, $\dfrac{1}{n^3}$.

$\displaystyle = \lim_{n \to \infty} \frac{1}{n^3} \left[\frac{n(n+1)(2n+1)}{6} \right]$ Use the formula for $\displaystyle\sum_{i=1}^{n} i^2$.

$\displaystyle = \lim_{n \to \infty} \frac{(n+1)(2n+1)}{6n^2}$ Reduce $\dfrac{n}{n^3} = \dfrac{1}{n^2}$.

$\displaystyle = \lim_{n \to \infty} \frac{2n^2 + 3n + 1}{6n^2}$ Multiply the numerator.

$\displaystyle = \lim_{n \to \infty} \frac{\dfrac{2n^2}{n^2} + \dfrac{3n}{n^2} + \dfrac{1}{n^2}}{\dfrac{6n^2}{n^2}}$ Divide each term by n^2

$\displaystyle = \lim_{n \to \infty} \frac{2 + \dfrac{3}{n} + \dfrac{1}{n^2}}{6}$ Reduce.

$\displaystyle = \frac{2 + 0 + 0}{6}$ Use $\displaystyle\lim_{n \to \infty} \frac{3}{n} = 0$ and

$\displaystyle\lim_{n \to \infty} \frac{1}{n^2} = 0.$

$\displaystyle = \frac{1}{3}$

5.3 APPROXIMATING AREA

Although we can find the area of many figures such as rectangles, trapezoids, circles, etc., we do not have a formula for finding the area bounded by a curve $y = f(x)$, the x-axis, and the vertical lines $x = a$ and $x = b$. However, we can make use of the formula for the area of a rectangle (length times width) to approximate such an area.

EXAMPLE 7

Find the shaded area using inscribed rectangles.

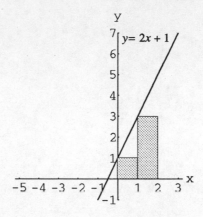

SOLUTION 7

Note that each shaded region is a rectangle of width 1. We can find the height of each rectangle by substituting the left endpoint of each interval into $y = 2x + 1$.

For [0, 1], height = 2(0) + 1 = 1
For [1, 2], height = 2(1) + 1 = 3
Shaded area = LW + LW
Shaded area = 1(1) + 3(1) = 4

EXAMPLE 8

Find the shaded area using circumscribed rectangles.

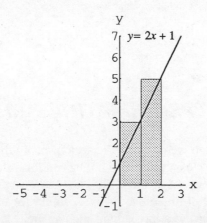

SOLUTION 8

These rectangles also have width 1. However, to find the heights, we now must use the right endpoint of each interval.

For [0, 1], height = 2(1) + 1 = 3

For [1, 2], height = 2(2) + 1 = 5

Shaded area = LW + LW

Shaded area = 3(1) + 5(1) = 8

The area we are really interested in (below $y = 2x + 1$ between $x = 0$ and $x = 2$) must be more than 4 and less than 8. We can improve our approximation by increasing the number of rectangles.

Here are some guidelines for approximating the area bounded by $y = f(x)$, $x = a$, $x = b$, and the x-axis, using n circumscribed or n inscribed rectangles.

1. Find the width of each rectangle using $w = \dfrac{b - a}{n}$.

2. Write out the intervals for *each* rectangle.

3. Find the length of each rectangle by substituting the left endpoint into $f(x)$ for inscribed rectangles and the right endpoint into $f(x)$ for circumscribed rectangles.

4. Multiply length times width to find the area of each rectangle.

5. Find the sum of the areas.

EXAMPLE 9

Approximate the area bounded by $f(x) = x^2 + 2$, x = 1, x = 3 and the x-axis using 4 inscribed rectangles.

SOLUTION 9

$$w = \frac{3 - 1}{4} = \frac{2}{4} = \frac{1}{2}$$
Find the width of each rectangle.

The rectangles are on $\left[1, \frac{3}{2}\right], \left[\frac{3}{2}, 2\right], \left[2, \frac{5}{2}\right], \left[\frac{5}{2}, 3\right]$.

For inscribed rectangles, use the left endpoint to find each height:

$f(1) = 1^2 + 2 = 3$

Substitute into
$f(x) = x^2 + 2.$

$f(\frac{3}{2}) = (\frac{3}{2})^2 + 2 = \frac{17}{4}$

$f(2) = 2^2 + 2 = 6$

$f(\frac{5}{2}) = (\frac{5}{2})^2 + 2 = \frac{33}{4}$

Find the area of each rectangle:

$3(\frac{1}{2}) = \frac{3}{2}$

$\frac{17}{4}(\frac{1}{2}) = \frac{17}{8}$

$6(\frac{1}{2}) = 3$

$\frac{33}{4}(\frac{1}{2}) = \frac{33}{8}$
_____

$\frac{43}{4}$

Find the sum of the areas.

By increasing the number of rectangles, we increase the accuracy of our approximation. In fact, if we let the number of rectangles approach infinity $(n \to \infty)$, we can actually find the area bounded by the curve, $x = a$, $x = b$, and the x-axis. We follow a procedure similar to the procedure for finding the sum with a finite number of rectangles.

To Find the Area as $(n \to \infty)$:

1. Find the width of each rectangle using $\Delta x = \dfrac{b-a}{n}$.

2. Find the area of the ith rectangle by finding $f(a + i\Delta x)\,\Delta x$.

3. Find $\displaystyle\lim_{n \to \infty} \sum_{i=1}^{n} f(a + i\Delta x)\,\Delta x$.

EXAMPLE 10

Find the area bounded by $f(x) = x^2 + 2$, x = 1, x = 2 and the x-axis.

SOLUTION 10

$$\Delta x = \frac{2-1}{n} = \frac{1}{n}$$

Find the width of each rectangle.

$$f(a + i\Delta x) = f(1 + i(\frac{1}{n}))$$

Find the height of the ith rectangle.

$$= f(1 + \frac{i}{n})$$

Simplify.

$$= (1 + \frac{i}{n})^2 + 2$$

Substitute into $f(x) = x^2 + 2$.

$$A = \lim_{n \to \infty} \sum_{i=1}^{n} \left[(1 + \frac{i}{n})^2 + 2 \right] \frac{1}{n}$$

Find the limit of the areas.

$$= \lim_{n \to \infty} \sum_{i=1}^{n} \left[1 + \frac{2i}{n} + \frac{i^2}{n^2} + 2 \right] \frac{1}{n}$$

$$= \lim_{n \to \infty} \sum_{i=1}^{n} \left[3 + \frac{2i}{n} + \frac{i^2}{n^2} \right] \frac{1}{n}$$

$$= \lim_{n \to \infty} \frac{1}{n} \sum_{i=1}^{n} \left[3 + \frac{2i}{n} + \frac{i^2}{n^2} \right]$$

Factor out the constant, $\frac{1}{n}$.

$$= \lim_{n \to \infty} \frac{1}{n} \left[\sum_{i=1}^{n} 3 + \sum_{i=1}^{n} \frac{2i}{n} + \sum_{i=1}^{n} \frac{i^2}{n^2} \right]$$

Use $\sum (ai + bi)$ $= \sum ai + \sum bi.$

$$= \lim_{n \to \infty} \frac{1}{n} \left[\sum_{i=1}^{n} 3 + \frac{2}{n} \sum_{i=1}^{n} i + \frac{1}{n^2} \sum_{i=1}^{n} i^2 \right]$$

Factor out each constant.

$$= \lim_{n \to \infty} \left[\frac{1}{n} \sum_{i=1}^{n} 3 + \frac{2}{n^2} \sum_{i=1}^{n} i + \frac{1}{n^3} \sum_{i=1}^{n} i^2 \right]$$

Multiply each term by $\frac{1}{n}$.

$$= \lim_{n \to \infty} \frac{1}{n} (3n) + 1 + \frac{1}{3} \qquad \text{See Example 6.}$$

$$= 3 + 1 + \frac{1}{3} = \frac{13}{3} \qquad \text{Add.}$$

Note that the technique shown here used the right endpoint to find the height of the ith rectangle. It can be shown that eiher the right or left end point can be used (or any point within the interval) to find the height.

5.4 THE DEFINITE INTEGRAL AND THE FUNDAMENTAL THEOREM OF CALCULUS

Definite Integrals

If we partition the interval so that our rectangles are *not* necessarily of equal width, and use any point in the subinterval to find the height of a rectangle, the sum of the areas of the rectangles is called a Riemann sum. The limit of this sum as the width of the widest rectangle approaches 0 is called a **definite integral**. Thus,

$$\int_a^b f(x)\,dx$$

is the definite integral of $f(x)$ from a to b, where a is the lower limit of integration and b is called the upper limit of integration. If $f(x)$ is a continuous, nonnegative function on $[a, b]$, then the area bounded by $f(x)$, $x = a$, $x = b$ and the x-axis equals

$$\int_a^b f(x)\,dx.$$

Fundamental Theorem of Calculus

The Fundamental Theorem of Calculus is the key to the relationship between indefinite and definite integrals and area under a curve. If we let $F(x) = f'(x)$, we know $\int F(x)\,dx = f(x) + c$. The Fundamental Theorem of Calculus states

$$\int_a^b F(x)\,dx = f(b) - f(a)$$

which means that we can find the area bounded by $y = F(x)$, $x = a$, $x = b$, and the x-axis by integrating $F(x)$, substituting in the upper and lower limits of integration and subtracting.

EXAMPLE 11

Evaluate each definite integral.

a) $\int_1^2 (x^2 + 2)\,dx$

b) $\int_0^3 x^6\,dx$

c) $\int_0^4 2\sqrt{x}\,dx$

SOLUTION 11

a) $\int_1^2 (x^2 + 2)\,dx = \left[\dfrac{x^{2+1}}{2+1} + 2x\right]\Big|_1^2$ Integrate.

$= \left[\dfrac{x^3}{3} + 2x\right]\Big|_1^2$ Simplify.

Now substitute $x = 2$, then $x = 1$ and subtract:

$= \left[\dfrac{(2)^3}{3} + 2\,(2)\right] - \left[\dfrac{(1)^3}{3} + 2\,(1)\right]$

$= (\dfrac{8}{3} + 4) - (\dfrac{1}{3} + 2)$

$= \dfrac{13}{3}$

b) $\int_0^3 x^6\,dx = \left[\dfrac{x^{6+1}}{6+1}\right]\Big|_0^3$ Integrate.

$$= \left[\frac{x^7}{7} \right] \Bigg|_0^3$$

Simplify.

$$= \frac{(3)^7}{7} - \frac{(0)^7}{7}$$

Evaluate by substituting $x = 3$, then $x = 0$ and subtracting.

$$= \frac{2187}{7} - 0 = \frac{2187}{7}$$

Simplify.

c) $$\int_0^4 2\sqrt{x}\,dx = 2\int_0^4 x^{1/2}\,dx$$

Rewrite $\sqrt{x}$ as $x^{1/2}$. Factor out the constant, 2.

$$= 2 \left[\frac{x^{\frac{1}{2}+1}}{\frac{1}{2}+1} \right] \Bigg|_0^4$$

Integrate using the Power Rule.

$$= 2 \left[\frac{x^{3/2}}{\frac{3}{2}} \right] \Bigg|_0^4$$

Simplify.

$$= 2 \left[\frac{2}{3} x^{3/2} \right] \Bigg|_0^4$$

$\dfrac{1}{3/2} = 1 \cdot \dfrac{2}{3} = \dfrac{2}{3}.$

$$= \frac{4}{3} [x^{3/2}] \Big|_0^4$$

Factor out the constant, $\dfrac{2}{3}$.

$$= \frac{4}{3} [4^{3/2} - 0^{3/2}]$$

Substitute $x = 4$, then $x = 0$ and subtract.

$$= \frac{4}{3} (4^{3/2}) = \frac{4}{3} \cdot 8 = \frac{32}{3}$$

Simplify.

Notice that our answer to Example 11a, $\dfrac{13}{3}$, is the same answer as Example 10. That is, we can find the area bounded by

$f(x) = x^2 + 2, x = 1, = 2$, and the x-axis by evaluating the definite integral

$$\int_{1}^{2} (x^2 + 2)\, dx.$$

Be careful to realize that this holds true (area = definite integral) only when the function is continuous and nonnegative.

Properties of Definite Integrals

There are several definitions and properties that can help you evaluate definite integrals.

$$\int_{a}^{a} f(x)\, dx = 0$$

$$\int_{a}^{b} f(x)\, dx = -\int_{b}^{a} f(x)\, dx \ \text{ for } a > b$$

$$\int_{a}^{b} f(x)\, dx = \int_{a}^{c} f(x)\, dx + \int_{c}^{b} f(x)\, dx \ \text{ if } f \text{ is integrable on an interval containing } a, b, \text{ and } c.$$

$$\int_{a}^{b} fk(x)\, dx = k\int_{a}^{b} f(x)\, dx$$

$$\int_{a}^{b} [f(x) + g(x)]\, dx = \int_{a}^{b} f(x)\, dx + \int_{a}^{b} g(x)\, dx$$

Note that the last two properties are restatements of our earlier properties for indefinite integrals.

EXAMPLE 12

Evaluate each definite integral.

a) $\displaystyle\int_3^3 (x^3 + 6x^2)\, dx$

b) $\displaystyle\int_2^{-1} x^2 dx$

SOLUTION 12

a) $\displaystyle\int_3^3 (x^3 + 6x^2)\, dx = 0$

There is no need to integrate and evaluate if you realize that the limits of integration are equal.

b) $\displaystyle\int_2^{-1} x^2 dx = -1 \int_{-1}^2 x^2 dx$

Use $\displaystyle\int_a^b f(x)\, dx = -\int_b^a f(x)\, dx$

$= -1 \left[\dfrac{x^{2+1}}{2+1} \right]\Bigg|_{-1}^2$

Integrate.

$= -1 \left[\dfrac{x^3}{3} \right]\Bigg|_{-1}^2$

Simplify.

$= -1 \left[\dfrac{(2)^3}{3} - \dfrac{(-1)^3}{3} \right]$

Evaluate.

$= -1 \left[\dfrac{8}{3} + \dfrac{1}{3} \right] = -3$

Finding Areas using Definite Integrals   When an area is bounded by a curve that is above the x-axis and the vertical lines $x = a$ and $x = b$, we can set up and evaluate the definite integral in a straightforward manner.

EXAMPLE 13

Find the area bounded by the given curve, the x-axis, and the lines $x = a$ and $x = b$.

a) $f(x) = 4x - x^2, x = 1, x = 3$

b) $f(x) = x^2 - 4x + 5, x = 1, x = 3$

SOLUTION 13

a) First sketch the region:

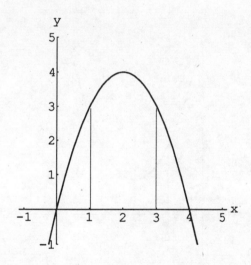

Set up the definite integral:

$$A = \int_{1}^{3} (4x - x^2)\, dx$$

$$= \left[\frac{4x^2}{2} - \frac{x^3}{3} \right]\Bigg|_{1}^{3} \qquad \text{Integrate.}$$

$$= \left[2x^2 - \frac{x^3}{3} \right]\Bigg|_{1}^{3} \qquad \text{Simplify.}$$

$$= (2\,(3)^2 - \frac{(3)^3}{3}) - (2\,(1)^2 - \frac{(1)^3}{3}) \quad \text{Evaluate.}$$

$$= (18 - 9) - (2 - \frac{1}{3}) \qquad\qquad \text{Simplify.}$$

$$= \frac{22}{3}$$

b) First sketch the region:

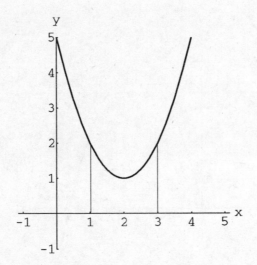

$$A = \int_{1}^{3} (x^2 - 4x + 5)\, dx \qquad\qquad \text{Set up the definite integral.}$$

$$= \left[\frac{x^3}{3} - 2x^2 + 5x \right]\Bigg|_{1}^{3} \qquad\qquad \text{Integrate.}$$

$$= \left[\frac{(3)^3}{3} - 2\,(3)^2 + 5\,(3) \right] - \left[\frac{1^3}{3} - 2\,(1)^2 + 5\,(1) \right]$$
$$\qquad\qquad\qquad\qquad\qquad\qquad \text{Evaluate.}$$

$$= (9 - 18 + 15) - (\frac{1}{3} - 2 + 5) \qquad\qquad \text{Simplify.}$$

$$= \frac{8}{3}$$

If the area bounded by the curve and the x-axis is *below* the x-axis, the value of the integral will be negative. In this case, use the negative of the integral to find the area. Note: area must always be positive even though an integral may be positive or negative.

EXAMPLE 14

Find the area bounded by the given function, $x = a$ and $x = b$.

a) $f(x) = -x^2, x = 0, x = 2$

b) $f(x) = \sin x, x = \pi, x = 2\pi$

SOLUTION 14

a) Consider the graph of $f(x) = -x^2$:

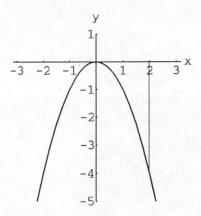

Since the area is bounded by the curve and the x-axis is below the x-axis, we use the negative of the integral:

$$A = -\int_0^2 (-x^2) \, dx \qquad \text{Set up the integral.}$$

$$= +\int_0^2 x^2 \, dx \qquad \text{Factor out the constant, } -1.$$

$$= \left[\frac{x^3}{3} \right]\Big|_0^2$$ Integrate.

$$= \frac{(2)^3}{3} - \frac{(0)^3}{3}$$ Evaluate.

$$= \frac{8}{3}$$ Simplify.

b) Sketch the graph of $f(x) = \sin x$:

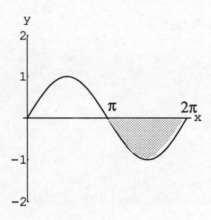

The shaded region is below the x-axis.

$$A = -\int_{\pi}^{2\pi} \sin x \, dx$$ Use the negative of the integral.

$$= -[-\cos x]\,\Big|_{\pi}^{2\pi}$$ Integrate.

$$= \cos x\,\Big|_{\pi}^{2\pi}$$ Factor out -1.

$$= \cos(2\pi) - \cos(\pi)$$ Evaluate.

$$= 1 - (-1)$$

$$= 2$$

If the area bounded by the function is partially above the x-axis and partially below, set up separate integrals for each region. Remember to take the negative of each region below the x-axis.

EXAMPLE 15

Find the area bounded by $f(x) = (x+2)^2 - 4$, $x = -1$, $x = 2$ and the x-axis.

SOLUTION 15

A sketch of the region shows that part of the area is below the x-axis and part of the area is above the x-axis:

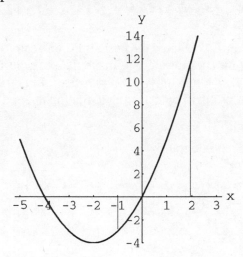

$$A = -\int_1^0 [(x+2)^2 - 4]\, dx + \int_0^2 [(x+2)^2 - 4]\, dx$$

$$= -\int_{-1}^0 (x^2 + 4x)\, dx + \int_0^2 (x^2 + 4x)\, dx \qquad \text{Simplify.}$$

$$= -\left[\frac{x^3}{3} + 2x^2 \right]\Bigg|_{-1}^0 + \left[\frac{x^3}{3} + 2x^2 \right]\Bigg|_0^2 \qquad \text{Integrate.}$$

$$= -\left[(\frac{0^3}{3} + 2\,(0)^2) - (\frac{(-1)^3}{3} + 2\,(-1)^2) \right] +$$

$$\left[(\frac{(2)^3}{3} + 2\,(2)^2) - (\frac{0^3}{3} + 2\,(0)^2) \right]$$

$$= -\left[0 - (-\frac{1}{3} + 2) \right] + \left[(\frac{8}{3} + 8) - 0 \right]$$

$$= -\left[-\frac{5}{3}\right] + \left[\frac{32}{3}\right]$$

$$= \frac{37}{3}$$

5.5 INTEGRATION BY SUBSTITUTION

In section 1, we stated the basic rules for integration. In this section we will select an appropriate u to make the problem fit one of our formulas. Note that if $u = f(x)$, $du = f'(x)dx$, where du is the differential of u. We begin each problem by selecting u, finding du, and substituting.

EXAMPLE 16

Evaluate each integral.

a) $\displaystyle\int (x^2 + 4)^5 (2x)\, dx$

b) $\displaystyle\int (x^3 + x^2)^8 (3x^2 + 2x)\, dx$

c) $\displaystyle\int 3 \cos 3x\, dx$

SOLUTION 16

a) Let $u = x^2 + 4$ Select u.

$du = 2x dx$ Find du.

Then $\displaystyle\int (x^2 + 4)^5 (2x)\, dx = \int u^5 du$ Substitute.

$$= \frac{u^6}{6} + c$$ Integrate using the Power Rule.

$$= \frac{(x^2 + 4)^6}{6} + c$$ Substitute for u.

b) Let $u = x^3 + x^2$ Select u.

$du = (3x^2 + 2x)\, dx$ Find du.

Then $\displaystyle\int (x^3 + x^2)^8 (3x^2 + 2x)\, dx = \int u^8 du$ Substitute.

$$= \frac{u^9}{9} + c$$ Integrate.

$$= \frac{(x^3 + x^2)^9}{9} + c \qquad\qquad \text{Substitute for } u.$$

c) Let $u = 3x$ — Select u.

$du = 3dx$ — Find du.

Then $\int 3\cos 3x\, dx = \int \cos 3x\,(3dx)$ — Rewrite.

$= \int \cos u\, du$ — Substitute.

$= \sin u + c$ — Integrate.

$= \sin(3x) + c$ — Substitute for u.

Producing du for the Power Rule

In the previous example, du was present in each integral. If we are missing a constant factor, we can often produce du by multiplying by a form of 1.

EXAMPLE 17

Evaluate each integral.

a) $\int (x^2 + 4)^5 x\, dx$

b) $\int \sqrt{4x + 1}\, dx$

c) $\int \frac{x}{(6x^2 + 3)^3} dx$

SOLUTION 17

a) Let $u = x^2 + 4$ — Select u.

$du = 2x\, dx$

We need $2x\, dx$. We have $x\, dx$. Multiply by $\frac{2}{2}$:

$\int (x^2 + 4)^5 x\, dx = \int (x^2 + 4)^5 \frac{2}{2} x\, dx$ — Multiply by $\frac{2}{2}$.

$= \frac{1}{2}\int (x^2 + 4)^5 2x\, dx$ — Factor out $\frac{1}{2}$.

$$= \frac{1}{2} \int u^5 du$$ 　　　　Substitute.

$$= \frac{1}{2} \cdot \frac{u^6}{6} + c$$ 　　　　Integrate using the Power Rule.

$$= \frac{1}{12} u^6 + c$$ 　　　　Simplify.

$$= \frac{1}{12} (x^2 + 4)^6 + c$$ 　　　　Substitute for u.

b) $$\int \sqrt{4x+1}\, dx = \int (4x+1)^{1/2}\, dx$$ 　　　　Rewrite the integrand.

Let $u = 4x + 1$ 　　　　Select u.

$du = 4dx$ 　　　　Find du.

We have dx. We need $4dx$. Multiply by $\frac{4}{4}$:

$$= \int (4x+1)^{1/2} \frac{4}{4} dx$$ 　　　　Multiply by $\frac{4}{4}$.

$$= \frac{1}{4} \int (4x+1)^{1/2} 4dx$$ 　　　　Factor out $\frac{1}{4}$.

$$= \frac{1}{4} \int u^{1/2} du$$ 　　　　Substitute.

$$= \frac{1}{4} \frac{u^{3/2}}{3/2} + c$$ 　　　　Integrate using the Power Rule.

$$= \frac{1}{4} \cdot \frac{2}{3} u^{3/2} + c$$ 　　　　Simplify.

$$= \frac{1}{6} (4x+1)^{3/2} + c$$ 　　　　Multiply $\frac{1}{4} \cdot \frac{2}{3} = \frac{1}{6}$. Substitute for u.

c) $$\int \frac{x}{(6x^2+3)^3} dx = \int (6x^2+3)^{-3} x\, dx$$ 　　　　Rewrite the integrand.

Let $u = 6x^2 + 3$ 　　　　Select u.

$$du = 12x \, dx \qquad\qquad \text{Find } du.$$

We have $x \, dx$. We need $12x \, dx$. Multiply by $\dfrac{12}{12}$:

$$= \int (6x^2 + 3)^{-3} \frac{12}{12} x \, dx \qquad\qquad \text{Multiply by } \frac{12}{12}.$$

$$= \frac{1}{12} \int (6x^2 + 3)^{-3} 12x \, dx \qquad\qquad \text{Factor out } \frac{1}{12}.$$

$$= \frac{1}{12} \int u^{-3} \, du \qquad\qquad \text{Substitute.}$$

$$= \frac{1}{12} \frac{u^{-2}}{-2} + c \qquad\qquad \text{Integrate using the Power Rule.}$$

$$= -\frac{1}{24u^2} + c \qquad\qquad \text{Simplify.}$$

$$= -\frac{1}{24 (6x^2 + 3)^2} + c \qquad\qquad \text{Substitute for } u.$$

Producing du for Trigonometric Functions

Recall our integration formulas involving trigonometric functions:

$$\int \sin u \, du = -\cos u + c$$

$$\int \cos u \, du = \sin u + c$$

$$\int \sec^2 u \, du = \tan u + c$$

Notice that the $\sin u$ and $\cos u$ are raised to an (understood) exponent of 1. The formula for integrating secants requires that the secant be squared. In these types of problems, u will be the angle of the trigonometric function.

EXAMPLE 18

Evaluate each integral.

a) $\displaystyle\int \sin 6x \, dx$

b) $\displaystyle\int \frac{\cos \sqrt{x}}{\sqrt{x}} \, dx$

c) $\int \sec^2(2\pi x)\, dx$

SOLUTION 18
a) $\int \sin 6x\, dx$

Let $u = 6x$	Let u equal the angle.
$du = 6dx$	Find du.

We have dx. We need $6dx$. Multiply by $\dfrac{6}{6}$:

$\displaystyle \int \sin 6x\, dx = \int \sin 6x\left(\frac{6}{6}\right) dx$ Multiply by $\dfrac{6}{6}$.

$\displaystyle = \frac{1}{6}\int \sin 6x\, 6dx$ Factor out $\dfrac{1}{6}$.

$\displaystyle = \frac{1}{6}\int \sin u\, du$ Substitute.

$\displaystyle = \frac{1}{6}\left[-\cos u\right] + c$ Integrate.

$\displaystyle = -\frac{1}{6}\cos(6x) + c$ Substitute for u.

b) $\displaystyle \int \frac{\cos\sqrt{x}}{\sqrt{x}}\, dx = \int \frac{\cos x^{1/2}}{x^{1/2}}\, dx$ Rewrite the integrand.

Let $u = x^{1/2}$	Let u equal the angle.
$du = \dfrac{1}{2}x^{-1/2}\, dx$	Find du.

We have $x^{-1/2}\, dx$. We need $\dfrac{1}{2}x^{-1/2}\, dx$. Multiply by $\dfrac{2}{2}$.

$\displaystyle = \int \frac{\cos x^{1/2}}{x^{1/2}} \cdot \frac{2}{2}\, dx$ Multiply by $\dfrac{2}{2}$.

$\displaystyle = 2\int \frac{\cos x^{1/2}}{2x^{1/2}}\, dx$ Factor out 2.

$\displaystyle = 2\int \cos u\, du$ Substitute.

$$= 2\sin u + c \qquad \text{Integrate.}$$

$$= 2\sin x^{1/2} + c \qquad \text{Substitute for } u.$$

c) Let $u = 2\pi x$ Let u equal the angle.

       $du = 2\pi dx$ 2π is a constant.

We have dx. We need $2\pi dx$. Multiply by $\dfrac{2\pi}{2\pi}$:

$$\int \sec^2 (2\pi x) \frac{2\pi}{2\pi} dx \qquad \text{Multiply by } \frac{2\pi}{2\pi}.$$

$$= \frac{1}{2\pi}\int \sec^2 (2\pi x)\, 2\pi dx \qquad \text{Factor out } \frac{1}{2\pi}.$$

$$= \frac{1}{2\pi}\int \sec^2 u\, du \qquad \text{Substitute.}$$

$$= \frac{1}{2\pi} \tan u + c \qquad \text{Integrate.}$$

$$= \frac{1}{2\pi} \tan (2\pi x) + c \qquad \text{Substitute for } u.$$

Trigonometric Functions Raised to Powers

If the exponent on $\sin u$ or $\cos u$ is *not* 1, the problem may be a form of the power rule. In this case, the integrand may appear to be a product involving sines and cosines. Note that in our list of basic integration formulas *there is no product rule*. Note also that it may help to write $\sin^n x$ as $(\sin x)^n$ to emphasize a power rule integration.

EXAMPLE 19

Use substitution to find each integral.

a) $\int \sin^4 x \cos x\, dx$

b) $\int \cos^3 2x \sin 2x\, dx$

SOLUTION 19

a) $\int \sin^4 x \cos x\, dx = \int (\sin x)^4 \cos x\, dx$

Let $u = \sin x$ Select u.

$du = \cos x \, dx$ Find du.

$\int (\sin x)^4 \cos x \, dx = \int u^4 \, du$ Substitute.

$= \dfrac{u^5}{5} + c$ Integrate.

$= \dfrac{(\sin x)^5}{5} + c$ Substitute for u.

$= \dfrac{1}{5} \sin^5 x + c$ Answer may be written in this form.

b) $\int \cos^3 2x \sin 2x \, dx = \int (\cos 2x)^3 \sin 2x \, dx$

Let $u = \cos 2x$ Select u.

$du = -2\sin 2x \, dx$ Find du.

We have $\sin 2x \, dx$. We need $-2\sin 2x$. Multiply by $\dfrac{-2}{-2}$.

$\int (\cos 2x)^3 \sin 2x \, dx = -\dfrac{1}{2} \int (\cos 2x)^3 (-2\sin 2x \, dx)$

$= -\dfrac{1}{2} \int u^3 \, du$ Substitute.

$= -\dfrac{1}{2} \cdot \dfrac{u^4}{4} + c$ Integrate.

$= -\dfrac{1}{8} u^4 + c$ Simplify.

$= -\dfrac{1}{8} [\cos 2x]^4 + c$ Substitute for u.

$= -\dfrac{1}{8} \cos^4 2x + c$ Answer may be written in this form.

Changing Limits of Integration   When we use substitution for a definite integral, we may either substitute, integrate, replace u and then evaluate or we may substitute, integrate, change the limits of integration, and evaluate. By changing the limits of integration, we avoid the step where we substitute for u. Compare the procedure for an example worked by both techniques.

EXAMPLE 20

Evaluate $\displaystyle\int_0^1 \frac{2x+4}{(x^2+4x+6)^2}\,dx$ without changing the limits of integration.

SOLUTION 20

Let $\quad u = x^2 + 4x + 6$ Select u.

Then $\quad du = (2x+4)\,dx$ Find du.

$$\int_0^1 \frac{2x+4}{(x^2+4x+6)^2}\,dx = \int \frac{du}{u^2}$$ Substitute.

$$= \int u^{-2}\,du$$ Simplify.

$$= \frac{u^{-1}}{-1}$$ Integrate.

$$= -\frac{1}{u}$$ Simplify.

$$= -\frac{1}{x^2+4x+6}$$ Substitute for u.

$$= -\frac{1}{x^2+4x+6}\Bigg|_0^1$$ Evaluate.

$$= -\frac{1}{1^2+4+6} - \left(-\frac{1}{0+0+6}\right)$$

$$= -\frac{1}{11} + \frac{1}{6} = \frac{5}{66}$$

EXAMPLE 21

Evaluate $\displaystyle\int_0^1 \frac{2x+4}{(x^2+4x+6)^2}\,dx$ by changing the limits of integration.

SOLUTION 21

We know $u = x^2 + 4x + 6$ and $du = (2x+4)dx$. Now we'll change the limits of integration from x values to u values.

When $x = 1$, $u = 1^2 + 4(1) + 6 = 11$

When $x = 0$, $u = 0^2 + 4(0) + 6 = 6$

The integral now becomes

$$\int_6^{11} u^{-2}\,du = -\frac{1}{u}\Big|_6^{11} \qquad\qquad \text{Integrate.}$$

$$= -\frac{1}{11} - \left(-\frac{1}{6}\right) \qquad\qquad \text{Evaluate.}$$

$$= -\frac{1}{11} + \frac{1}{6} = \frac{5}{66}$$

Of course, both techniques lead to the same correct answer. Generally it will be up to you to choose the technique you prefer.

*T*his *chapter introduced integration as the inverse process of differentiation. We concentrated on eight basic integration formulas introduced in section 1. We also discussed the application of integration to finding the area bounded by a function, the x-axis and two vertical lines. We used the Fundamental Theorem of Calculus to evaluate definite integrals. Finally, we began to examine the use of substitution to help us integrate functions that fit our basic eight formulas after an appropriate substitution.*

Practice Exercises

1. Find each integral.

(a) $\int 2\,dx$

(b) $\int 3x^4\,dx$

(c) $\int (x^2 - x^3)\,dx$

2. Integrate.

(a) $\int \frac{1}{x^5}\,dx$

(b) $\int \sqrt[3]{x^2}\,dx$

(c) $\int \left(\frac{2x^2 + x^5}{x}\right)\,dx$

(d) $\int \sqrt[3]{x}\,(x - \sqrt{x})\,dx$

3. Integrate.

(a) $\int 3\cos x\,dx$

(b) $\int (6\sin x - 2\cos x)\,dx$

(c) $\int (\sec^2 x - 2x)\,dx$

4. Find the indicated sums.

(a) $\displaystyle\sum_{j=1}^{6} (j^2 + 2)$

(b) $\displaystyle\sum_{i=3}^{6} 2i$

(c) $\displaystyle\sum_{i=1}^{3} (i + k)$

5. Use the summation formulas to find each sum.

(a) $\displaystyle\sum_{i=1}^{100} 3i$

(b) $\displaystyle\sum_{i=1}^{100} 2i^2$

(c) $\displaystyle\sum_{i=1}^{200} (2i + 5)$

6. Find each limit.

(a) $\displaystyle\lim_{n\to\infty} \sum_{i=1}^{n} \frac{32i}{n^2}$

(b) $\displaystyle\lim_{n\to\infty} \sum_{i=1}^{n} \frac{4}{n} + \frac{8i}{n^2} + \frac{8i^2}{n^3}$

7. Approximate the area bounded by the given functions using 4 inscribed rectangles.

(a) $f(x) = 2x$, $x = 0$, $x = 4$ and the x-axis.

(b) $f(x) = x^2 + 1$, $x = 1$, $x = 3$ and the x-axis.

8. Use the limit process to find the area bounded by

(a) $f(x) = 2x$, $x = 0$, $x = 4$ and the x-axis.

(b) $f(x) = x^2 + 1$, $x = 1$, $x = 3$ and the x-axis.

9. Evaluate each definite integral.

(a) $\displaystyle\int_{1}^{3} (2x^2 + 1)\,dx$

(b) $\displaystyle\int_0^1 x^3\,dx$

(c) $\displaystyle\int_0^8 3\sqrt[3]{x}\,dx$

10. Evaluate each definite integral.

(a) $\displaystyle\int_{-1}^{-1} (2x^3+3x+1)\,dx$

(b) $\displaystyle\int_1^{-2} (3x+1)\,dx$

11. Find the area bounded by the given curve, the x-axis, and the lines $x=a$ and $x=b$.

(a) $f(x) = x^2-2x+3 \quad x=1, x=4.$

(b) $f(x) = -x^2-8x \quad x=-4, x=0.$

12. Find the area bounded by the given function, $x=a$ and $x=b$.

(a) $f(x) = x^3 \quad x=-2, x=0.$

(b) $f(x) = \cos x \quad x=\pi/2, x=3\pi/2.$

13. Find the area bounded by
$f(x) = -x^3-x^2+2x, x=-2, x=1.$

14. Find the area bounded by $f(x) = \dfrac{1}{2}\sin x,$
$x=0, x=3\pi/2.$

15. Evaluate each integral.

(a) $\displaystyle\int (2x^3+5)^4(6x^2)\,dx$

(b) $\displaystyle\int (3x^4-2x^3)^{-3}(12x^3-6x^2)\,dx$

(c) $\displaystyle\int 2\sin 2x\,dx$

16. Evaluate each integral.

(a) $\displaystyle\int \sqrt{2x-5}\,dx$

(b) $\displaystyle\int (x^4-3)^3 x^3\,dx$

(c) $\displaystyle\int \dfrac{x^2}{(4x^3+1)^5}\,dx$

17. Evaluate each integral.

(a) $\displaystyle\int \cos 4x\,dx$

(b) $\displaystyle\int 3\sec^2 2x\,dx$

(c) $\displaystyle\int x\sin(4x^2)\,dx$

18. Use substitution to find each integral.

(a) $\displaystyle\int \sin^2 x\cos x\,dx$

(b) $\displaystyle\int \sqrt{\cos 4x}\,\sin 4x\,dx$

(c) $\displaystyle\int \tan^{-4} x\sec^2 x\,dx$

19. Evaluate, changing limits of integration when convenient.

(a) $\displaystyle\int_0^2 (x^6+4x^3)^2(6x^5+12x^2)\,dx$

(b) $\displaystyle\int_0^{\frac{\pi}{10}} \sin^2 5x\cos 5x\,dx$

Answers

1.

(a) $2x + c$

(b) $\dfrac{3}{5}x^5 + c$

(c) $\dfrac{1}{3}x^3 - \dfrac{1}{4}x^4 + c$

2.

(a) $-\dfrac{1}{4}x^{-4} + c$

(b) $\dfrac{3}{5}x^{5/3} + c$

(c) $x^2 + \dfrac{1}{5}x^5 + c$

(d) $\dfrac{3}{7}x^{7/3} - \dfrac{6}{11}x^{11/6} + c$

3.

(a) $3\sin x + c$

(b) $-6\cos x - 2\sin x + c$

(c) $\tan x - x^2 + c$

4.

(a) 103

(b) 36

(c) $6 + 3k$

5.

(a) 15,150

(b) 676,700

(c) 41,200

6.

(a) 16

(b) 32/3

7.

(a) 12

(b) 35/4

8.

(a) 16

(b) 32/3

9.

(a) 58/3

(b) 1/4

(c) 36

10.

(a) 0 (note limits of integration)

(b) 3/2

11.

(a) 15

(b) 128/3

12.

(a) 4

(b) 2

13. 37/12

14. 3/2

15.

(a) $\dfrac{1}{5}(2x^3+5)^5+c$

(b) $-\dfrac{1}{2}(3x^4-2x^3)^{-2}+c$

(c) $-\cos 2x+c$

16.

(a) $\dfrac{1}{3}(2x-5)^{3/2}+c$

(b) $\dfrac{1}{16}(x^4-3)^4+c$

(c) $-\dfrac{1}{48(x^4-3)^4}+c$

17.

(a) $\dfrac{1}{4}\sin 4x+c$

(b) $\dfrac{3}{2}\tan 2x+c$

(c) $-\dfrac{1}{8}\cos(4x^2)+c$

18.

(a) $\dfrac{1}{3}\sin^3 x+c$

(b) $-\dfrac{1}{6}(\cos 4x)^{3/2}+c$

(c) $-\dfrac{1}{3}\tan^{-3}x+c$

19.

(a) 294,912

(b) 1/15

6

Applications of Integration

In this chapter we will investigate a few of the applications involving integration. We have already discovered that the area bounded by a curve and the x-axis can be found by integrating the function. We shall extend this idea to finding the area between two curves, to finding volumes formed by revolving curves about a line, to finding the lengths of curves and more. The key idea to these problems will be to examine a slice of the figure (whether it involves an area, volume, arc length, etc.) and to relate the shape of that slice to figures which are already familiar to us.

6.1 AREA BETWEEN CURVES

If two functions f and g are continuous, and $f(x) \geq g(x)$, we can find the area bounded by f and g, and the vertical lines $x = a$ and $x = b$ by

$$\int_a^b [f(x) - g(x)] \, dx$$

The location of f and g can be totally or partially above or below the x-axis without affecting the formula. We must be careful that $f(x) \geq g(x)$ on $[a, b]$. We can state some guidelines for finding the area between two curves.

Finding the Area Between $f(x)$ and $g(x)$

1. Sketch the graph of $f(x)$ and $g(x)$.
2. If the area is not bounded by $x = a$ and $x = b$, set $f(x) = g(x)$ an solve for the intersection points or use substitution to solve the two equations in two unknowns.
3. If vertical slices are bounded above by $f(x)$ and below by $g(x)$, use

$$\text{Area} = \int_{x_1}^{x_2} [f(x) - g(x)]\, dx$$

4. If horizontal slices are bounded on the right by $f(x)$ and the left by $g(x)$, solve each equation for x, and use

$$\text{Area} = \int_{y_1}^{y_2} [f(y) - g(y)]\, dy$$

Note: When using dx slices, remember to use (top minus bottom) to find the height of a slice and x-coordinates for the limits of integration, and when using dy slices, remember to use (right minus left) to find the height of a slice and y-coordinates for the limits of integration.

Vertical Slices

EXAMPLE 1

Find the area bounded by $f(x) = 3x - 2$ and $g(x) = x^2$.

SOLUTION 1

Sketch the graph:

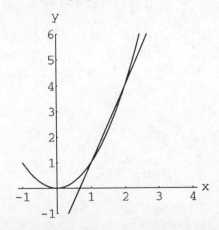

Since the area is bounded by the two curves, we'll find their intersection points:

$$3x - 2 = x^2 \qquad \text{Set } f(x) = g(x).$$

$$x^2 - 3x + 2 = 0 \qquad \text{This is a quadratic equation.}$$

$$(x - 2)(x - 1) = 0 \qquad \text{Factor.}$$

$$x = 2 \quad \text{or} \quad x = 1 \qquad \text{Set each factor equal to 0 and solve for } x.$$

The points of intersection are (2, 4) and (1, 1).

Since each vertical slice is bounded above by $f(x) = 3x - 2$ and below by $g(x) = x^2$, set up the integral using x-coordinates for the limits of integration

as:

$$A = \int_1^2 [(3x - 2) - (x^2)]\, dx \qquad \text{Use top} - \text{bottom.}$$

$$= \int_1^2 (3x - 2 - x^2)\, dx \qquad \text{Simplify.}$$

$$= \left. \frac{3x^2}{2} - 2x - \frac{x^3}{3} \right|_1^2 \qquad \text{Integrate.}$$

$$= \left[\frac{3(2)^2}{2} - 2(2) - \frac{(2)^3}{3} \right] - \left[\frac{3(1)^2}{2} - 2(1) - \frac{(1)^3}{3} \right]$$

$$= (6 - 4 - \frac{8}{3}) - (\frac{3}{2} - 2 - \frac{1}{3})$$

$$= \frac{1}{6}$$

Therefore the area bounded by the two functions is $\frac{1}{6}$.

Horizontal slices   **EXAMPLE 2**
Find the area of the region bounded by $x = 4 - y^2$ and $y = \frac{1}{2}x - \frac{1}{2}$.

SOLUTION 2
Sketch the graph:

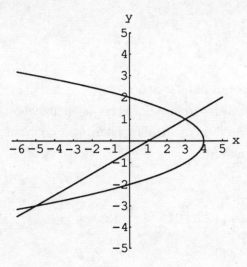

Note that if we try to draw vertical slices, some slices will go from $x = 4 - y^2$ to itself:

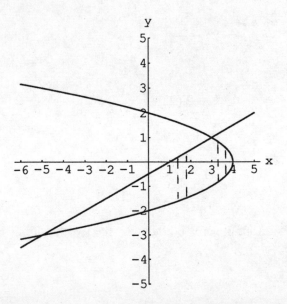

Therefore, we must use horizontal slices:

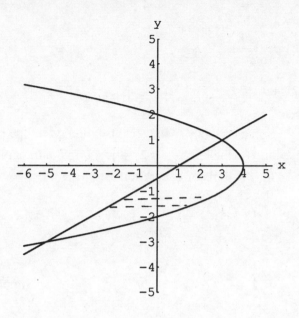

Since both equations are *not* solved for y, it will be easier to find the intersection points by substitution:

$$y = \frac{1}{2}x - \frac{1}{2}$$

$$y = \frac{1}{2}(4 - y^2) - \frac{1}{2}$$ Substitute $x = 4 - y^2$.

$$2y = 4 - y^2 - 1$$ Multiply by 2 to clear fractions.

$$y^2 + 2y - 3 = 0$$ Solve the quadratic equation.

$$(y + 3)(y - 1) = 0$$ Factor.

$$y = -3 \quad \text{or} \quad y = +1$$ Set each factor equal to 0 and solve.

The points of intersection are (–5, –3) and (3, 1).

We are using horizontal slices, so we must solve each equation for x:

$$y = \frac{1}{2}x - \frac{1}{2} \qquad x = 4 - y^2 \qquad \text{Solve each equation for } x.$$

$$2y = x - 1$$

$$2y + 1 = x$$

Since each horizontal slice is bounded on the right by $x = 4 - y^2$ and on the left by $x = 2y + 1$, set up the integral using y-coordinates for the limitsof integration as:

$$A = \int_{-3}^{1} [\,(4 - y^2) - (2y + 1)\,]\, dy$$

$$= \int_{-3}^{1} (-y^2 - 2y + 3)\, dy \qquad \text{Simplify.}$$

$$= \left[-\frac{y^3}{3} - y^2 + 3y \right]\Bigg|_{-3}^{1} \qquad \text{Integrate.}$$

$$= \left[-\frac{(1)^3}{3} - (1)^2 + 3\,(1) \right] - \left[\frac{-(-3)^3}{3} - (-3)^2 + 3\,(-3) \right]$$

$$= \left(\frac{5}{3} \right) - (-9)$$

$$= \frac{32}{3}$$

Setting up Two Integrals

If $f(x) \le g(x)$ for x in $[a, b]$ but $f(x) \ge g(x)$ for x in $[b, c]$, two integrals will be needed to find the area bounded by the curves on $[a, c]$. A carefully drawn sketch will help you determine which curve is on top.

EXAMPLE 3

Find the area of the region bounded by $f(x) = \sin x$, $g(x) = \cos x$, $x = 0$ and

$$x = \frac{5\pi}{4}.$$

SOLUTION 3

Sketch the graph:

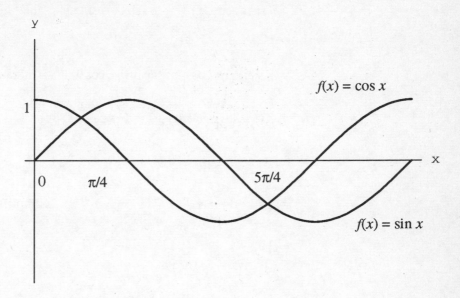

We can find the intersection points on $[0, \frac{5\pi}{4}]$ by setting $f(x) = g(x)$ and solving.

$\sin x = \cos x$	Set $f(x) = g(x)$.
$\dfrac{\sin x}{\cos x} = \dfrac{\cos x}{\cos x}$	Divide both sides by $\cos x$.
$\tan x = 1$	Use $\dfrac{\sin x}{\cos x} = \tan x$.
$x = \dfrac{\pi}{4}$ and $x = \dfrac{5\pi}{4}$	$\tan x$ is positive in quadrants I and III.

Notice that $\cos x$ is on top from $[0, \frac{\pi}{4}]$ and that $\sin x$ is on top from $[\frac{\pi}{4}, \frac{5\pi}{4}]$.

Using vertical slices for both integrals we have:

$$A = \int\limits_{0}^{\frac{\pi}{4}} [\cos x - \sin x]\, dx + \int\limits_{\frac{\pi}{4}}^{\frac{5\pi}{4}} [\sin x - \cos x]\, dx$$

$$= (\sin x + \cos x)\,|_0^{\frac{\pi}{4}} + (-\cos x - \sin x)\,|_{\frac{\pi}{4}}^{\frac{5\pi}{4}} \quad \text{Integrate.}$$

$$= \left[(\sin\frac{\pi}{4} + \cos\frac{\pi}{4}) - (\sin 0 + \cos 0) \right] \quad \text{Evaluate.}$$

$$+ \left[(-\cos\frac{5\pi}{4} - \sin\frac{5\pi}{4}) - (-\cos\frac{\pi}{4} - \sin\frac{\pi}{4}) \right]$$

$$= \left[(\frac{\sqrt{2}}{2} + \frac{\sqrt{2}}{2}) - (0 + 1) \right] + \left[-(\frac{-\sqrt{2}}{2}) - (\frac{-\sqrt{2}}{2}) - (\frac{-\sqrt{2}}{2} - \frac{\sqrt{2}}{2}) \right]$$

$$= [\sqrt{2} - 1] + [\sqrt{2} + \sqrt{2}] \qquad\qquad \text{Simplify.}$$

$$= 3\sqrt{2} - 1$$

6.2 VOLUME USING DISCS AND WASHERS

Solids of Revolution   A solid of revolution is a solid formed by revolving a plane region about a line. Hold up a piece of paper, revolve it around one edge - the resulting right circular cylinder is a solid of revolution.

The Disc Method   One method for finding the volume of a solid of revolution is called the disc method. Once a solid has been formed, imagine slicing through it perpendicular to its axis of revolution. If the slice is a solid disc (a record without a hole), the disc method is an appropriate choice. The formula is based on the formula for the area of a circle, πr^2.

Finding Volume Using the Disc Method
1. If the function is revolved about $y = 0$, set up the integral

$$V = \pi \int_{x_1}^{x_2} [f(x)]^2 dx$$

2. If the function is revolved about $x = 0$, solve the given function for $x = g(y)$ and set up the integral

$$V = \pi \int_{y_1}^{y_2} [g(y)]^2 dy$$

EXAMPLE 4

Find the volume of the solid formed by revolving the region bounded by $f(x) = 4 - x^2$, $x = 0$, $y = 0$ about the x–axis.

SOLUTION 4

Since the equation of the x-axis is $y = 0$, we use procedure #1. We find the limits of integration by sketching the plane region $f(x) = 4 - x^2$ and determining the x-coordinates where the discs begin and end:

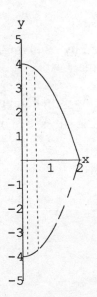

Since the region is bounded by $x = 0$, and intersects the x-axis at $x = 2$, we set up the following integral:

$$V = \pi \int_0^2 (4 - x^2)\, dx$$

$$= \pi \int_0^2 (16 - 8x^2 + x^4)\, dx \qquad \text{Square the function.}$$

$$= \pi \left[16x - \frac{8x^3}{3} + \frac{x^5}{5} \right]\Bigg|_0^2 \qquad \text{Integrate.}$$

$$= \pi \left[(16\,(2) - \frac{8\,(2)^3}{3} + \frac{(2)^5}{5}) - (16\,(0) - \frac{8\,(0)^3}{3} + \frac{(0)^5}{5}) \right]$$
$$\text{Evaluate.}$$

$$= \pi \left[(32 - \frac{64}{3} + \frac{32}{5}) - (0) \right] \qquad \text{Simplify.}$$

$$= \pi \cdot \frac{256}{15} \quad \text{or} \quad \frac{256\pi}{15}$$

EXAMPLE 5

Find the volume of the solid formed by revolving the region bounded by $f(x) = 4 - x^2$, $x = 0$, $y = 0$ about the y-axis.

SOLUTION 5

Note that this is the same plane region as in Example 4, but now it is revolved about $x = 0$ (the y-axis). The slices are now dy slices (horizontal slices):

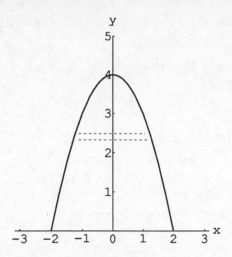

We must solve $y = 4 - x^2$ for x:

$$y - 4 = -x^2$$ Given equation.

$$-y + 4 = x^2$$ Multiply both sides by -1.

$$+\sqrt{-y + 4} = x$$ Take the square root of both sides.

Note that we use only the positive square root because the original function was defined with $x \geq 0$. Set up the integral using y-coordinates for the limits of integration:

$$V = \pi \int_0^4 \left(\sqrt{-y + 4}\right)^2 dy$$

$$= \pi \int_0^4 (-y + 4) \, dy$$ Square the expression.

$$= \pi \left[-\frac{y^2}{2} + 4y\right]\Bigg|_0^4$$ Integrate.

$$= \pi \left[\left(-\frac{(4)^2}{2} + 4(4) \right) - \left(-\frac{0^2}{2} + 4(0) \right) \right] \text{Evaluate.}$$

$$= \pi [(8) - (0)] \qquad\qquad\qquad \text{Simplify.}$$

$$= 8\pi$$

EXAMPLE 6

Find the volume of the solid formed by revolving the region bounded by $f(x) = 4 - x^2$, $y = 1$, $x = 0$, about $y = 1$.

SOLUTION 6

First sketch the plane region:

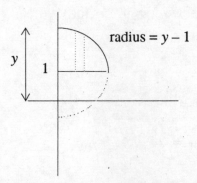

Notice that the radius of a disc is no longer y, but $y - 1$. Since we will be using dx slices, we must use a function solved for y.

$$y - 1 = (4 - x^2) - 1 \qquad\qquad \text{Use } y = 4 - x^2.$$

$$y - 1 = 3 - x^2$$

The limits of integration are from $x = 0$ to where $f(x) = 4 - x^2$ and $y = 1$
intersect:

$$4 - x^2 = 1 \qquad\qquad\qquad \text{Set } f(x) = y.$$

$$-x^2 = -3 \qquad\qquad\qquad \text{Solve for } x.$$

$$x^2 = 3$$

$$x = \pm\sqrt{3}$$

We will use the positive square root since we are working in quadrant I.

$$V = \pi \int_{0}^{\sqrt{3}} (3 - x^2)^2 \, dx \qquad \text{Set up the integral.}$$

$$= \pi \int_{0}^{\sqrt{3}} (9 - 6x^2 + x^4) \, dx \qquad \text{Square the binomial.}$$

$$= \pi \left[9x - 2x^3 + \frac{1}{5} x^5 \right] \Big|_{0}^{\sqrt{3}} \qquad \text{Integrate.}$$

$$= \pi \left[(9(\sqrt{3}) - 2(\sqrt{3})^3 + \frac{1}{5}(\sqrt{3})^5) - 0 \right] \text{Evaluate.}$$

$$= \pi \left[9\sqrt{3} - 6\sqrt{3} + \frac{9}{5}\sqrt{3} \right] \qquad \text{Simplify.}$$

$$= \pi \frac{24\sqrt{3}}{5} \quad \text{or} \quad \frac{24\pi\sqrt{3}}{5} \qquad \text{Add similar terms.}$$

The Washer Method

When revolving a region about a line leaves a hole in the slice, we use the washer method to find the volume of the solid of revolution:

$$V = \pi \int_{x_1}^{x_2} [(R(x))^2 - (r(x))^2] \, dx \qquad \text{Revolved about } y = c.$$

$$V = \pi \int_{y_1}^{y_2} [(R(y))^2 - (r(y))^2] \, dy \qquad \text{Revolved about } x = b.$$

where R is the length of the outer radius and r is the length of the inner radius.

EXAMPLE 7

Find the volume of the solid formed by revolving the region bounded by $f(x) = 4 - x^2, y = 1, x = 0$ about the x-axis.

SOLUTION 7

First sketch the plane region:

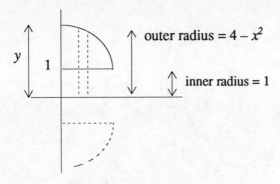

Note that the washers start at $x = 0$ and end at $x = \sqrt{3}$ (see Example 6). The volume is then

$$V = \pi \int_0^{\sqrt{3}} \left[(4 - x^2)^2 - (1)^2 \right] dx$$

$$= \pi \int_0^{\sqrt{3}} (16 - 8x^2 + x^4 - 1)\, dx \qquad \text{Simplify.}$$

$$= \pi \int_0^{\sqrt{3}} (15 - 8x^2 + x^4)\, dx \qquad \text{Combine similar terms.}$$

$$= \pi \left[15x - \frac{8x^3}{3} + \frac{x^5}{5} \right]\Bigg|_0^{\sqrt{3}} \qquad \text{Integrate.}$$

$$= \pi \left[\left(15\sqrt{3} - \frac{8(\sqrt{3})^3}{3} + \frac{(\sqrt{3})^5}{5} \right) - (0) \right] \text{Evaluate.}$$

$$= \pi \left(15\sqrt{3} - 8\sqrt{3} + \frac{9\sqrt{3}}{5} \right) \qquad \text{Simplify.}$$

$$= \pi \left(\frac{44}{5} \sqrt{3} \right) \quad \text{or} \quad \frac{44\pi\sqrt{3}}{5} \qquad \text{Simplify.}$$

6.3 VOLUME BY SHELLS

Another method for finding volumes of solids of revolution is the **shell method**. Try to imagine sliding a soup can (both ends open, no soup) into the solid of revolution. We find the volume using $2\pi rh$ where r represents the distance from the axis of revolution out to the shell, and h represents the height of the shell. We have the following two formulas for the shell method:

$$V = 2\pi \int_{x_1}^{x_2} r(x) \, h(x) \, dx \qquad \text{Revolved about } x = b.$$

$$V = 2\pi \int_{y_1}^{y_2} r(y) \, h(y) \, dy \qquad \text{Revolved about } y = c.$$

EXAMPLE 8

Find the volume of the solid of revolution formed by revolving the region bounded by $y = x^2 + 2$, $x = 1$, $x = 0$ and $y = 0$ about $x = 0$ (the y-axis).

SOLUTION 8

Sketch the plane region:

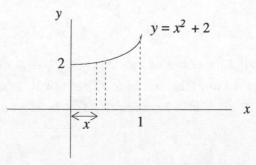

The radius of each shell is x, the height is $h(x) = x^2 + 2$ and the radii of the shells go from $x = 0$ to $x = 1$. The volume is

$$V = 2\pi \int_0^1 x\,(x^2 + 2)\,dx$$

$$= 2\pi \int_0^1 (x^3 + 2x)\,dx \qquad\qquad \text{Simplify.}$$

$$= 2\pi \left(\frac{x^4}{4} + x^2\right)\bigg|_0^1 \qquad\qquad \text{Integrate.}$$

$$= 2\pi\left[\left(\frac{1}{4} + 1\right) - (0)\right] \qquad\qquad \text{Evaluate.}$$

$$= 2\pi\left(\frac{5}{4}\right) = \frac{5}{2}\pi \qquad\qquad \text{Simplify.}$$

EXAMPLE 9

Find the volume of the solid of revolution formed by revolving the region bounded by $y = x^2 + 2$, $x = 1$, $x = 0$ and $y = 0$ about $x = 2$.

SOLUTION 9

Sketch the plane region:

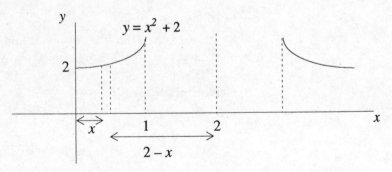

Note that the radius of a shell is now $2 - x$, since the radius must be measured from the axis of revolution (in this case, $x = 2$). The height is still $h(x) = x^2 + 2$, the radii of the shells go from $x = 0$ to $x = 1$, so the volume is

$$V = 2\pi \int_0^1 (2 - x)\,(x^2 + 2)\,dx$$

$$= 2\pi \int_0^1 (2x^2 + 4 - x^3 - 2x)\, dx \qquad \text{Simplify.}$$

$$= 2\pi \left[\frac{2x^3}{3} + 4x - \frac{x^4}{4} - x^2 \right] \Big|_0^1 \qquad \text{Integrate.}$$

$$= 2\pi \left[\left(\frac{2}{3} + 4 - \frac{1}{4} - 1\right) - (0) \right] \qquad \text{Evaluate.}$$

$$= \frac{41\pi}{6} \qquad \text{Simplify.}$$

dy Shells

If the region is revolved about $y = c$, for c a constant, we will need shells whose radii are measured along the y-axis, and heights that must be written in terms of $x = f(y)$. Study the following example.

EXAMPLE 10

Find the volume of the solid of revolution formed by revolving the region bounded by $y = \sqrt{x}$, $x = 0$ and $y = 2$ about the line $y = 4$.

SOLUTION 10
Sketch the plane region:

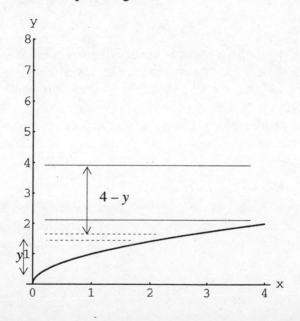

The radii are measured from the axis of revolution ($y = 4$), and so $r(y) = 4 - y$. The height must be given in terms of y, so

$$y = \sqrt{x}$$ Given function.

$$y^2 = x$$ Solve for x.

The radii of the shells run from $y = 0$ to $y = 2$, so the volume is

$$V = 2\pi \int_0^2 (4 - y)\,(y^2)\,dy$$

$$= 2\pi \int_0^2 (4y^2 - y^3)\,dy$$ Simplify.

$$= 2\pi\,(\frac{4y^3}{3} - \frac{y^4}{4})\,\Big|_0^2$$ Integrate.

$$= 2\pi \left[(\frac{32}{3} - \frac{16}{4}) - (0) \right]$$ Evaluate.

$$= \frac{40}{3}\pi$$ Simplify.

Comparing the Disc and Shell Methods Many of the volumes for solids of revolution can be found by using either method. If a typical slice involves finding a distance from a curve to itself (for either a radius or height measurement), then choose the other method. Sometimes one method will be more convenient, either because the resulting integral is easier to calculate, or because one integral can be used instead of two.

EXAMPLE 11

Revolve the indicated region about the indicated line to form a solid of revolution. Then set up the integral to find the volume using both the disc and shell method. If one method is not possible, indicate why.

(a) $y = -(x - 2)^2 + 4$, $y = 0$ about $y = 0$.

(b) $y = -(x-2)^2 + 4$, $y = 0$ about $x = 0$.

(c) $y = -x^2 + 4$, $y = 1$, $x = 0$ about $y = 0$.

SOLUTION 11

a)   Sketch the indicated region.

By discs:

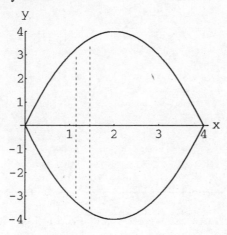

$$V = \pi \int_0^4 [-(x-2)^2 + 4] \, dx$$

By shells:

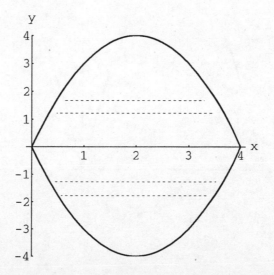

We cannot find the height of a shell because we are measuring from the curve to itself.

b) $y = -(x-2)^2 + 4$, $y = 0$ about $x = 0$

By washers:

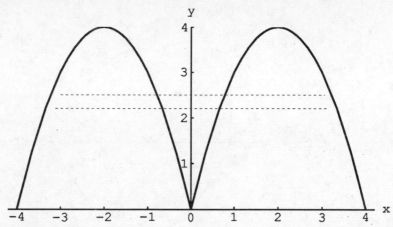

We cannot use washers because a radius would have to be measured from the curve to itself.

By shells:

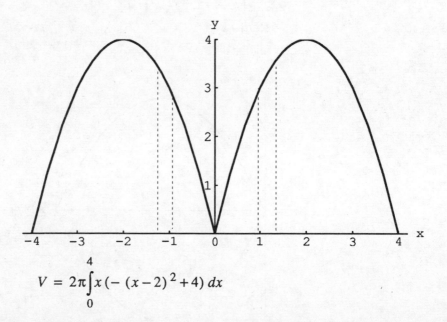

$$V = 2\pi \int_0^4 x(-(x-2)^2+4)\,dx$$

c) $y = -x^2 + 4$, $y = 1$, $x = 0$ about $y = 0$

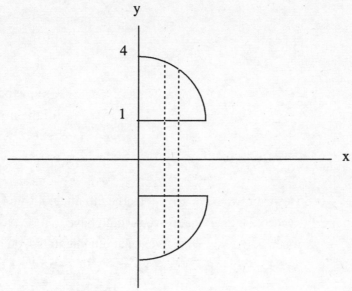

By washers:

$$V = \pi \int\limits_{0}^{\sqrt{3}} [\, (-x^2 + 4)^2 - (1)^2] \, dx$$

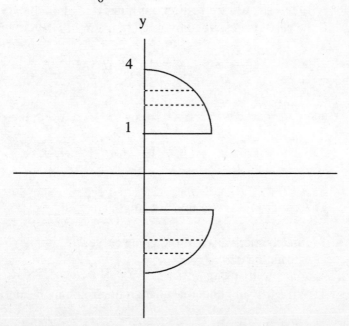

By shells:

To find $h(y)$, solve $y = -x^2 + 4$ for x:

$$y - 4 = -x^2$$

$$4 - y = x^2$$

$$\sqrt{4 - y} = x$$

Use the positive square root for the first Quadrant curve.

$$V = 2\pi \int_1^4 y\,(\sqrt{4 - y})\,dy$$

However, we have not yet learned to integrate $y\sqrt{4 - y}$, and if we needed a numerical answer, would have to resort to the washer method. (If you wish to check both integrals, you may use $\int y\sqrt{4 - y}\,dy = -\frac{2}{3}y\,(4 - y)^{3/2} - \frac{4}{15}\,(4 - y)^{5/2} + c$).

6.4 LENGTH OF A CURVE

In this section we restrict our interest to smooth curves of finite length. If the curve is described by $y = f(x)$, $a \leq x \leq b$, the arc length L is

$$L = \int_a^b \sqrt{1 + [f'(x)]^2}\,dx$$

and if the curve is described by $x = g(y)$, $c \leq y \leq d$, the arc length L is

$$L = \int_c^d \sqrt{1 + [g'(y)]^2}\,dy$$

The steps to follow to find arc length are:

1. Find the derivative of the given curve.
2. Square the derivative.
3. Add 1 to that square.
4. Write the sum under a square root. You may need to factor and use

$$\sqrt{(p+q)^2} = p+q.$$

5. Integrate.
6. Evaluate.

EXAMPLE 12

Find the arc length of $f(x) = x^{3/2} + 2$ on $[1, 4]$.

SOLUTION 12

$f(x) = x^{3/2} + 2$	Given function.
$f'(x) = \dfrac{3}{2}x^{1/2}$	Find the derivative.
$[f'(x)]^2 = \left[\dfrac{3}{2}x^{1/2}\right]^2$	Square the derivative.
$= \dfrac{9}{4}x$	Simplify.
$\sqrt{1 + [f'(x)]^2} = \sqrt{1 + \dfrac{9}{4}x}$	Add 1 and write the sum under a square root.
$L = \displaystyle\int_1^4 \sqrt{1 + \dfrac{9}{4}x}\,dx$	Set up the integral.
$= \dfrac{4}{9}\displaystyle\int_1^4 \left(1 + \dfrac{9}{4}x\right)^{1/2} \left(\dfrac{9}{4}dx\right)$	If $u = \dfrac{9}{4}x$, $du = \dfrac{9}{4}dx$
$= \dfrac{4}{9}\cdot\dfrac{2}{3}\left[1 + \dfrac{9}{4}x\right]^{3/2}\Bigg|_1^4$	Integrate.
$= \dfrac{8}{27}\left[\left(1 + \dfrac{9}{4}(4)\right)^{3/2} - \left(1 + \dfrac{9}{4}(1)\right)^{3/2}\right]$	Evaluate.
$= \dfrac{8}{27}\left[10^{3/2} - \left(\dfrac{13}{4}\right)^{3/2}\right]$	Simplify.

EXAMPLE 13

Find the arc length of $f(x) = \dfrac{x^4}{8} + \dfrac{1}{4x^2}$ on $[1, 4]$.

SOLUTION 13

$f(x) = \dfrac{x^4}{8} + \dfrac{1}{4x^2}$ 　　　　　　　　　Given function.

$f'(x) = \dfrac{1}{2}x^3 - \dfrac{1}{2}x^{-3}$ 　　　　　　　$\dfrac{1}{4x^2} = \dfrac{1}{4}x^{-2}$.

$\quad = \dfrac{x^3}{2} - \dfrac{1}{2x^3}$ 　　　　　　　　　Simplify.

$\quad = \dfrac{x^6 - 1}{2x^3}$ 　　　　　　　　　　　Combine fractions.

$[f'(x)]^2 = \left(\dfrac{x^6 - 1}{2x^3}\right)^2$ 　　　　　　Square derivative.

$\quad = \dfrac{x^{12} - 2x^6 + 1}{4x^6}$ 　　　　　　Square the numerator and the denominator.

$1 + [f'(x)]^2 = 1 + \dfrac{x^{12} - 2x^6 + 1}{4x^6}$ 　　Add 1.

$\quad = \dfrac{4x^6}{4x^6} + \dfrac{x^{12} - 2x^6 + 1}{4x^6}$ 　　Combine fractions using $4x^6$ as LCD.

$\quad = \dfrac{x^{12} + 2x^6 + 1}{4x^6}$ 　　　　　Add the numerators.

$\quad = \dfrac{(x^6 + 1)^2}{(2x^3)^2}$ 　　　　　　　Factor.

Then arc length, L, is

$$L = \int_{1}^{4} \sqrt{\frac{(x^6 + 1)^2}{(2x^3)^2}}\, dx$$

Write the sum under a square root.

$$= \int_{1}^{4} \frac{x^6 + 1}{2x^3}\, dx$$

Simplify.

$$= \int_{1}^{4} \left(\frac{x^3}{2} + \frac{1}{2x^3} \right) dx$$

Split the fraction.

$$= \left[\frac{x^4}{8} - \frac{1}{4} x^{-2} \right] \Big|_{1}^{4}$$

$$\int \frac{1}{2x^3}\, dx = \frac{1}{2} \int x^{-3}\, dx.$$

$$= \left(\frac{(4)^4}{8} - \frac{1}{4(4)^2} \right) - \left(\frac{(1)^4}{8} - \frac{1}{4(1)^2} \right)$$

Evaluate.

$$= (32 - \frac{1}{64}) - (\frac{1}{8} - \frac{1}{4})$$

Simplify.

$$= \frac{2055}{64} \quad \text{or} \quad 32\frac{7}{64}$$

Simplify.

EXAMPLE 14

Set up the integral that represents the arc length of $y = \sin x$ on $[0, \frac{\pi}{2}]$.

SOLUTION 14

$y = \sin x$

Given curve.

$y' = \cos x$

Find the derivative.

$(y')^2 = \cos^2 x$

Square the derivative.

$(y')^2 + 1 = \cos^2 x + 1$

Add 1.

$$L = \int_{0}^{\pi/2} \sqrt{\cos^2 x + 1}\, dx$$

Set up the integral.

6.5 AREA OF A SURFACE OF REVOLUTION

If we revolve a plane smooth curve about a line, we form a **surface of revolution**. The formula for finding the area of the surface of revolution makes use of the arc length formulas from section 6.4. The arc length must be multiplied by $2\pi r$, where r is the distance from the axis of revolution to the curve.

Area of a Surface of Revolution

If the curve is given as $y = f(x)$ on $[a,b]$, then the area of the surface formed by revolving the curve about a line is

$$S = 2\pi \int_a^b (r(x) \sqrt{1 + [f'(x)]^2})\, dx$$

where $r(x)$ is the distance from the axis of revolution to $f(x)$.

If the curve is given as $x = g(y)$ on $[c, d]$, then the area of the surface formed by revolving the curve about a line is

$$S = 2\pi \int_c^d (r(y) \sqrt{1 + [g'(y)]^2})\, dy$$

where $r(y)$ is the distance from the axis of revolution to $g(y)$.

EXAMPLE 15

Find the area of the surface formed by revolving
$f(x) = x^3$ on $[0, 1]$ about the x-axis.

SOLUTION 15
A sketch will help us find $r(x)$:

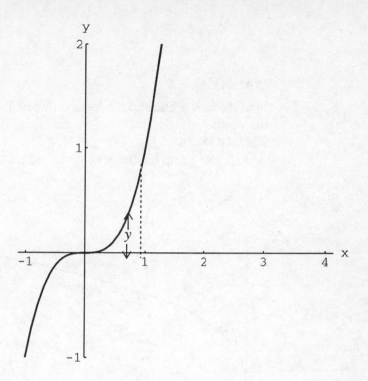

This distance from the x-axis to the curve is y, which equals x^3. Thus,

$$S = 2\pi \int_0^1 x^3 \sqrt{1 + \left(3x^2\right)^2}\, dx \qquad\qquad f(x) = x^3, f(x) = 3x^2.$$

$$= 2\pi \int_0^1 x^3 \left(1 + 9x^4\right)^{1/2} dx \qquad\qquad \text{Let } u = 9x^4,\, du = 36x^3\, dx.$$

$$= 2\pi \frac{1}{36} \int_0^1 36x^3 \left(1 + 9x^4\right)^{1/2} dx \qquad\qquad \text{Multiply inside by 36, and}$$
$$\text{outside by } \frac{1}{36}.$$

$$= \frac{\pi}{18} \left[\frac{2}{3} \left(1 + 9x^4\right)^{3/2} \right]\Big|_0^1 \qquad\qquad \text{Integrate.}$$

$$= \frac{\pi}{27} \left[\left(1 + 9(1)^4\right)^{3/2} - \left(1 + 9(0)^4\right)^{3/2} \right] \text{ Evaluate.}$$

$$= \frac{\pi}{27} \left(10^{3/2} - 1\right) \qquad\qquad \text{Simplify.}$$

EXAMPLE 16

Find the area of the surface formed by revolving $x = y^3, 0 \le y \le 1$ about the y-axis.

SOLUTION 16

A sketch will help us find $r(y)$:

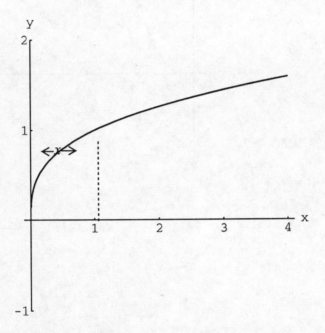

The distance from the y-axis to the curve is x, which equals y^3, so the area of the surface is

$$S = 2\pi \int_0^1 y^3 \sqrt{1 + (3y^2)^2} \, dy \qquad\qquad g(y) = y^3, \, g'(y) = 3y^2.$$

Notice that this is the exact same integral as Example 15, with y's rather than x's. So,

$$S = \frac{\pi}{27} \left(10^{3/2} - 1\right)$$

EXAMPLE 17

Set up, but do not evaluate, the integral necessary to find the area of the surface formed by revolving $f(x) = \sin x$ on $[0, \pi/2]$ about the x-axis.

SOLUTION 17

We previously found the integral representing the arc length for $y = \sin x$ in Example 14. We need only find $r(x)$:

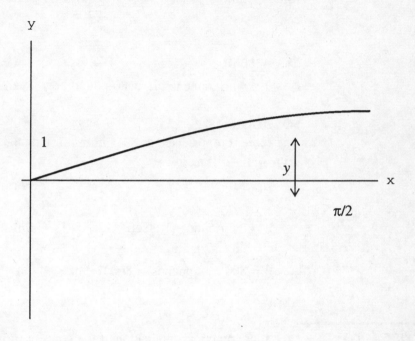

The distance from the x-axis to the curve is y, which equals $\sin x$. So the surface area is

$$S = 2\pi \int_{0}^{\frac{\pi}{2}} \sin x \sqrt{1 + \cos^2 x}\, dx$$

6.6 WORK

Constant Force

We begin our discussion of work by examining work done by a constant force. In this case, the work done to move an object a distance x by a force F is

$$W = Fx$$

EXAMPLE 18

Find the work done to lift an 80-pound bag of cement 10 feet.

SOLUTION 18

The force is represented as 80 pounds. The distance the bag is moved, 10 feet, is x. Thus

$W = Fx$ Formula for work.

$W = (80\text{ pounds})(10\text{ feet})$ Substitute.

$W = 800$ foot pounds or 800 ft $\cdot$ lbs

Varying Force

A more practical application of the concept of work involves a varying force, such as the work to compress or stretch a spring or the work to move a liquid. In these cases, work is defined as an integral where $F(x)$ describes the varying force used to move an object from a to b. Thus

$$W = \int_{a}^{b} F(x)\, dx$$

Springs

We'll use Hooke's Law to find the force to compress or stretch a spring

$$F(x) = kx$$

where k is the spring constant (a number that remains constant for a given spring) and x is the distance the spring is stretched or compressed from its natural length.

To Find Work Done Using Springs
1. Find k, the spring constant (if not already given) by substituting a given force F and distance x into $F = kx$.
2. Find the limits of integration by determining the distance over which the work is to be measured.

EXAMPLE 19

A force of 5 pounds compresses a spring 2 inches from its natural length of 14 inches. Find the work done in compressing the spring a total of 6 inches.

SOLUTION 19

$F = kx$ Find k using $F = kx$.

$5 = k(2)$ $F = 5, x = 2$.

$\dfrac{5}{2} = k$

The spring is to be compressed 6 inches, which means the work starts at a distance of $x = 0$, and ends when $x = 6$. Note that the spring will now be $14 - 6 = 8$ inches long.

$W = \displaystyle\int_{0}^{6} \dfrac{5}{2} x \, dx$ Set up the integral.

$= \dfrac{5}{4} x^2 \Big|_{0}^{6}$ Integrate.

$= \dfrac{5}{4} (6^2 - 0^2)$ Evaluate.

$= 45 \text{ in} \cdot \text{lb}$

EXAMPLE 20

A force of 4 kilograms stretches a spring 2.5 centimeters. How much work must be done to stretch the spring and additional 2 centimeters?

SOLUTION 20

$F = kx$ Find k using $F = kx$.

$$4 = k(2.5) \qquad\qquad\qquad F = 4, x = 2.5.$$

$$1.6 = k \qquad\qquad\qquad \frac{4}{2.5} = 1.6$$

The spring is to be stretched an *additional* 2 centimeters, which means we want to find the work done from $x = 2.5$ to $x = (2.5 + 2) = 4.5$.

$$W = \int_{2.5}^{4.5} 1.6x\,dx \qquad\qquad \text{Set up the integral.}$$

$$= \frac{1.6x^2}{2}\Big|_{2.5}^{4.5} \qquad\qquad \text{Integrate.}$$

$$= 0.8\,[\,(4.5)^2 - (2.5)^2\,] \qquad\qquad \text{Evaluate.}$$

$$= 11.2 \text{ cm} \cdot \text{kg}$$

Moving Liquids

We can find the work done to move a liquid using the same idea as springs. We must find the force needed to move the liquid, which will generally equal the weight of the liquid times the volume of a typical slice, and the distance the liquid is to move.

EXAMPLE 21

A cylindrical tank of diameter 16 feet and height of 10 feet is filled with water. Find the work done to pump the water over the top edge of the tank.

SOLUTION 21

A sketch will help us visualize the situation:

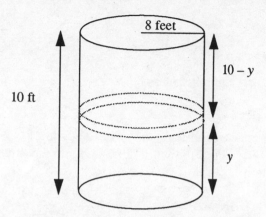

Each slice is a disc whose volume is $\pi r^2 \Delta y$ where Δy is the thickness of a slice. Since the diameter was given as 16 feet, the radius, r, is 8 feet.

$$V = \pi (8)^2 \Delta y = 64 \pi \Delta y \text{ ft}^3$$

The force needed to move a slice is the weight of a slice. Since the weight of water is 62.4 pounds per cubic foot, we have

$$F = (62.4 \frac{\text{lb}}{\text{ft}^3}) \ (64 \pi \Delta y \text{ft}^3)$$

$$= 3993.6 \pi \Delta y \text{lb}$$

A slice at height y must move a distance of $10 - y$ feet, so

$$W = \int_0^{10} 3993.6 \pi \ (10 - y) \ dy \qquad\qquad W = \int \text{Force} \cdot \text{Distance}$$

$$= 3993.6 \pi \int_0^{10} (10 - y) \ dy \qquad\qquad \text{Simplify.}$$

$$= 3993.6 \pi \left[10y - \frac{y^2}{2} \right]\Bigg|_0^{10} \qquad\qquad \text{Integrate.}$$

$$= 3993.6\pi\left[\,(10\,(10) - \frac{10^2}{2}) - (0)\right] \quad \text{Evaluate.}$$

$$= 199{,}680\pi \ \ \text{ft} \cdot \text{lb}$$

$$\approx 627{,}313 \ \text{ft} \cdot \text{lb}$$

EXAMPLE 22

The same cylindrical tank as in Example 21 is filled with liquid weighing 42 lb/ft^3. Find the work done to pump the liquid 6 feet above the top of the tank.

SOLUTION 22

Let's begin with a sketch:

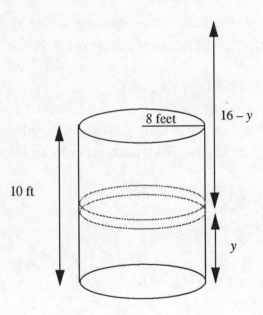

We must change the weight of a slice to 42 lb/ft^3, and the distance each slice must move $(16 - y)$. Note that the slices still go from 0 (at the bottom of the tank) to 10 (at the top of the tank).

$$F = (42 \ \text{lb/ft}^3)\,(64\pi\Delta y \text{ft}^3)$$

$$= 2688\pi\Delta y \ \text{lb}$$

$$W = \int_{0}^{10} (2688\pi dy)(16 - y) \qquad\qquad W = \int \text{force} \cdot \text{distance}.$$

$$= 2688\pi \int_{0}^{10} (16 - y)\, dy \qquad\qquad \text{Simplify.}$$

$$= 2688\pi \left[16y - \frac{y^2}{2} \right]\Bigg|_{0}^{10} \qquad\qquad \text{Integrate.}$$

$$= 2688\pi \left[(16(10) - \frac{10^2}{2}) - (0) \right] \qquad \text{Evaluate.}$$

$$= 2688\pi(110) \qquad\qquad \text{Simplify.}$$

$$= 295680\pi \ \text{ft} \cdot \text{lb}$$

$$\approx 928906 \ \text{ft} \cdot \text{lb}$$

6.7 Fluid Force

Several laws govern our work with fluid force. First, the pressure exerted by a fluid on a surface is the same at all points at a given depth (or elevation). Next, the fluid force on a horizontal surface with area A equals the density of the fluid times the depth of the surface times the area of the surface. By considering slices of a submerged vertical surface, we can find the fluid force on the entire surface using

$$F = \delta \int_{y_1}^{y_2} h \cdot L dy$$

where δ is the density of the fluid, h is the depth of the fluid at a horizontal slice of length L. The limits of integration are the y-coordinates of the bottom and top of the vertical surface. Some guidelines to solving fluid force problems are:

1. Draw a sketch. Impose x- and y-axes in a convenient place on your sketch.
2. Draw a horizontal slice on your sketch to help determine the depth

and length of a slice as indicated by your x- and y-axes.
3. Set up the force integral.
4. Integrate and evaluate.

EXAMPLE 23

The vertical end of a tank filled with water has the shape of a rectangle as shown below. If the depth of the water is 3 feet, find the total force against the end of the tank.

Note, $\delta = 62.4$ pounds per cubic foot.

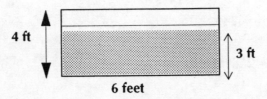

SOLUTION 23

We place our x- and y-axes as follows:

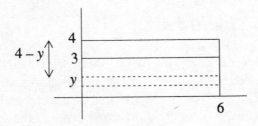

The depth of a slice is $4 - y$.

The length of a slice is 6.

Thus,

$$F = 62.4\int_{0}^{3} (4 - y)\,(6)\,dy \qquad\qquad F = \delta\int hL\,dy$$

$$= 62.4\int_{0}^{3} (24 - 6y)\,dy \qquad\qquad \text{Simplify.}$$

$$= 62.4 \left[24y - 3y^2\right]\Big|_0^3 \qquad\qquad \text{Integrate.}$$

$$= 62.4 \left[24\,(3) - 3\,(3)^2 - 0\right] \qquad\qquad \text{Evaluate.}$$

$$= 2808 \text{ pounds}$$

EXAMPLE 24

Find the fluid force on the given vertical plate submerged in water.

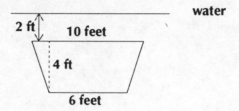

SOLUTION 24

We can place the x-axis at the water line and the y-axis in the middle of the plate:

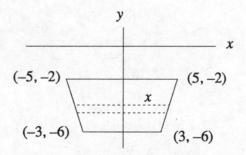

The length of a slice is $2x$. We find an expression for x in terms of y by finding the equation of the line that contains $(5, -2)$ and $(3, -6)$.

$$m = \frac{-2 - (-6)}{5 - 3} \qquad\qquad\qquad m = \frac{y_2 - y_1}{x_2 - x_1}$$

$m = 2$ Simplify.

$y - (-2) = 2(x - 5)$ $y - y_1 = m(x - x_1)$

$y + 2 = 2x - 10$ Simplify.

$y + 12 = 2x$ Solve for x.

$\dfrac{1}{2}y + 6 = x$

The length of a slice is:

$2x = 2(\dfrac{1}{2}y + 6) = y + 12$

We find force:

$F = 62.4 \displaystyle\int_{-6}^{-2} (-y)(y + 12)\, dy$ $F = \delta \int hL\,dy.$

$= 62.4 \displaystyle\int_{-6}^{-2} (-y^2 - 12y)\, dy$ Simplify.

$= 62.4 \left[-\dfrac{y^3}{3} - 6y^2 \right] \Big|_{-6}^{-2}$ Integrate.

$= 62.4 \left[(-\dfrac{(-2)^3}{3} - 6(-2)^2) - (-\dfrac{(-6)^3}{3} - 6(-6)^2) \right]$

$= 62.4 \left[(\dfrac{8}{3} - 24) - (\dfrac{216}{3} - 216) \right]$

$= 62.4 \left[\dfrac{368}{3} \right] \approx 7654.4$ pounds

EXAMPLE 25

A swimming pool is 16 feet wide, 60 feet long, 4 feet deep at one end and 8 feet deep at the other end. Find the fluid force against one of the 60 foot walls when the pool is filled with water.

SOLUTION 25

Placing the deep end of the pool along the y-axis, we can sketch the following:

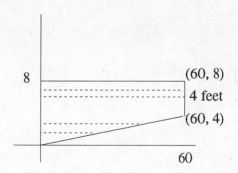

Note that we have two types of slices in our sketch, slices from $0 \le y \le 4$ and slices from $4 \le y \le 8$.

When $0 \le y \le 4$, the length of a slice is x. To find an expression for x in terms of y, find the equation of the line containing $(0, 0)$ and $(60, 4)$:

$$m = \frac{4-0}{60-0} = \frac{4}{60} = \frac{1}{15} \qquad\qquad m = \frac{y_2 - y_1}{x_2 - x_1}.$$

$$y - 0 = \frac{1}{15}(x - 0) \qquad\qquad y - y_1 = m(x - x_1).$$

$$y = \frac{1}{15}x \qquad\qquad \text{Simplify.}$$

$$15y = x \qquad\qquad \text{Solve for } x.$$

Thus the fluid force for $0 \le y \le 4$ is

$$F = 62.4 \int_0^4 (8 - y)(15y)\, dy \qquad\qquad F = \delta \int hL\, dy.$$

$$= 62.4 \int_0^4 (120y - 15y^2)\, dy \qquad\qquad \text{Simplify.}$$

$$= 62.4 \left[60y^2 - 5y^3 \right]\Big|_0^4 \qquad\qquad \text{Integrate.}$$

$$= 62.4 \left[(60(4)^2 - 5(4)^3) - (0) \right] \qquad\qquad \text{Evaluate.}$$

$= 62.4\,[960 - 320] = 39936$ pounds

When $4 \le y \le 8$, the length of a slice is 60 feet and so

$$F = 62.4 \int_{4}^{8} (8 - y)\,(60)\,dy \qquad\qquad F = \delta \int hL\,dy.$$

$$= 62.4 \int_{4}^{8} (480 - 60y)\,dy \qquad\qquad \text{Simplify.}$$

$$= 62.4\,[480y - 30y^2]\Big|_{4}^{8} \qquad\qquad \text{Integrate.}$$

$$= 62.4\,[\,(480\,(8) - 30\,(8)^2) - (480\,(4) - 30\,(4)^2)\,]$$

$$= 62.4\,[\,(3840 - 1920) - (1920 - 480)\,]$$

$$= 62.4\,[480] = 29952 \text{ pounds}$$

The total fluid force is the sum of the forces or

$$F = 39936 + 29952 = 69{,}888 \text{ pounds}$$

6.8 MOMENTS AND CENTROIDS

Center of Mass in One Dimension

If you have ever played on a seesaw, you know that in order for the seesaw to balance, both the weights and distances from the fulcrum must be "right." The physical law that governs this relationship is

$$m_1 d_1 = m_2 d_2 \quad \text{or} \quad m_1 d_1 - m_2 d_2 = 0$$

Expanding this idea to masses $m_1, m_2, m_3, \dots, m_n$ at respective distances $x_1, x_2, x_3, \dots, x_n$, from the origin, we define the **moment about**

the origin as

$$M = m_1 x_1 + m_2 x_2 + m_3 x_3 + \ldots + m_n x_n$$

and the **center of mass** as

$$\bar{x} = \frac{M}{m} \text{ where } m = m_1 + m_2 + m_3 + \ldots + m_n$$

EXAMPLE 26

Find the center of mass for a system with $m_1 = 6$ at $x_1 = 3$, $m_2 = 4$ at $x_2 = -5$ and $m_3 = 10$ at $x_3 = 5$.

SOLUTION 26

$$M = m_1 x_1 + m_2 x_2 + m_3 x_3 \qquad \qquad \text{Find the moment.}$$

$$M = 6\,(3) + (4)\,(-5) + (10)\,(5) \qquad \text{Substitute.}$$

$$= 18 - 20 + 50 = 48$$

$$m = m_1 + m_2 + m_3 \qquad \qquad \qquad \text{Find the total mass.}$$

$$m = 6 + 4 + 10 = 20 \qquad \qquad \qquad \text{Substitute and add.}$$

$$\bar{x} = \frac{M}{m} \qquad \qquad \qquad \qquad \qquad \text{Find the center of mass.}$$

$$\bar{x} = \frac{48}{20} = 2.8 \qquad \qquad \qquad \qquad \text{Substitute.}$$

This means the system would balance if we put the fulcrum at $x = 2.8$.

Center of Mass in Two Dimensions

We can extend the idea of center of mass if we consider points in a plane rather than points on an x-axis. If we have masses $m_1, m_2, m_3, \ldots, m_n$ at points $(x_1, y_1), (x_2, y_2), (x_3, y_3), \ldots, (x_n, y_n)$, then

$$M_y = m_1 x_1 + m_2 x_2 + m_3 x_3 + \ldots + m_n x_n \qquad \text{Moment about } y\text{-axis}$$

$$M_x = m_1 y_1 + m_2 y_2 + m_3 y_3 + \ldots + m_n y_n \qquad \text{Moment about } x\text{-axis}$$

$$(\bar{x}, \bar{y}) = (\frac{M_y}{m}, \frac{M_x}{m}) \qquad \text{Center of mass where}$$
$$m = m_1 + m_2 + m_3 + \ldots + m_n$$

EXAMPLE 27

Find the center of mass for a system with $m_1 = 5$ at $(2, 3)$, $m_2 = 8$ at $(-3, -1)$, $m_3 = 4$ at $(-1, 6)$ and $m_4 = 3$ at $(1, -2)$.

SOLUTION 27

$$M_y = m_1 x_1 + m_2 x_2 + m_3 x_3 + \ldots + m_n x_n \qquad \text{Find the moment about the } y\text{-axis.}$$

$$M_y = 5\,(2) + 8\,(-3) + 4\,(-1) + 3\,(1)$$

$$M_y = 10 - 24 - 4 + 3 = -15$$

$$M_x = m_1 y_1 + m_2 y_2 + m_3 y_3 + \ldots + m_n y_n \qquad \text{Find the moment about the } x\text{-axis.}$$

$$M_x = 5\,(3) + 8\,(-1) + 4\,(6) + 3\,(-2)$$

$$M_x = 15 - 8 + 24 - 6 = 25$$

$$m = m_1 + m_2 + m_3 + m_4 \qquad \text{Find the total mass.}$$

$$m = 5 + 8 + 4 + 3 = 20$$

$$(\bar{x}, \bar{y}) = (\frac{M_y}{m}, \frac{M_x}{m}) \qquad \text{Find the center of mass.}$$

$$(\bar{x}, \bar{y}) = (\frac{-15}{20}, \frac{25}{20}) \qquad \text{Substitute.}$$

$$(\bar{x}, \bar{y}) = (-\frac{3}{4}, \frac{5}{4}) \qquad \text{Reduce.}$$

Planar Lamina

The previous examples dealt with masses at points on a line or in the plane. We wish to extend the idea of center of mass to thin flat plates with uniform density called planar lamina. To find the moments and center of mass, we use the following formulas, where $f(x)$ and $g(x)$ are continuous functions and the lamina has uniform density δ.

If a planar lamina of density δ is bounded by $f(x)$ and $g(x)$, $a \le x \le b$,

$$M_x = \frac{\delta}{2} \int_a^b [f^2(x) - g^2(x)] \, dx \qquad \text{Moment about } x\text{-axis.}$$

$$M_y = \delta \int_a^b x [f(x) - g(x)] \, dx \qquad \text{Moment about } y\text{-axis.}$$

$$(\bar{x}, \bar{y}) = (\frac{M_y}{m}, \frac{M_x}{m}) \qquad \text{Center of mass.}$$

where $m = \delta \int_a^b [f(x) - g(x)] \, dx$.

EXAMPLE 28

Find the moments and the center of mass for the planar lamina of density δ bounded by $f(x) = \sqrt{x}$ and $g(x) = x^2$.

SOLUTION 28

We find where the curves intersect by setting them equal to each other and solving.

$$\sqrt{x} = x^2$$

$$(\sqrt{x})^2 = (x^2)^2 \qquad \text{Square both sides.}$$

$$x = x^4 \qquad \text{Simplify.}$$

$$0 = x^4 - x \qquad \text{Get 0 on one side.}$$

$$0 = x(x^3 - 1) \qquad \text{Common factor.}$$

$$0 = x(x-1)(x^2 + x + 1) \qquad \text{Factor the difference of two cubes.}$$

$$x = 0 \quad x = 1 \qquad \text{Set each factor equal to 0 and solve.}$$

Find the moment about the *x*-axis:

$$M_x = \frac{\delta}{2} \int_0^1 [\, (\sqrt{x})^2 - (x^2)^2 \,] \, dx \qquad \text{Set up the integral.}$$

$$= \frac{\delta}{2} \int_0^1 (x - x^4) \, dx \qquad \text{Simplify.}$$

$$= \frac{\delta}{2} \left[\frac{x^2}{2} - \frac{x^5}{5} \right] \Big|_0^1 \qquad \text{Integrate.}$$

$$= \frac{\delta}{2} \left[\, (\frac{1}{2} - \frac{1}{5}) - (0) \, \right] \qquad \text{Evaluate.}$$

$$= \frac{\delta}{2} \cdot \frac{3}{10} = \frac{3\delta}{20} \qquad \text{Simplify.}$$

Find the moment about the *y*-axis:

$$M_y = \delta \int_0^1 x \, [\, \sqrt{x} - x^2 \,] \, dx \qquad \text{Set up the integral.}$$

$$= \delta \int_0^1 (x^{3/2} - x^3) \, dx \qquad x\sqrt{x} = x \cdot x^{1/2} = x^{3/2}.$$

$$= \delta \left[\frac{2}{5} x^{5/2} - \frac{x^4}{4} \right] \Big|_0^1 \qquad \text{Integrate.}$$

$$= \delta \left[\, (\frac{2}{5}(1) - \frac{1}{4}) - (0) \, \right] \qquad \text{Evaluate.}$$

$$= \delta (\frac{3}{20}) = \frac{3}{20} \delta \qquad \text{Simplify.}$$

Find the mass of the lamina:

$$m = \delta \int_a^b [\, f(x) - g(x) \,] \qquad \text{Formula for mass.}$$

$$= \delta \int_0^1 [\, \sqrt{x} - x^2 \,] \, dx \qquad \text{Set up the integral.}$$

$$= \delta \left[\frac{2}{3} x^{3/2} - \frac{x^3}{3} \right] \Big|_0^1 \quad \sqrt{x} = x^{1/2}.$$ Integrate.

$$= \delta \left[\left(\frac{2}{3}(1) - \frac{1}{3} \right) - (0) \right]$$ Evaluate.

$$= \delta \left[\frac{1}{3} \right] = \frac{1}{3} \delta$$

Now find the center of mass:

$$(\bar{x}, \bar{y}) = \left(\frac{M_y}{m}, \frac{M_x}{m} \right)$$ Formula for center of mass.

$$(\bar{x}, \bar{y}) = \left(\frac{\frac{3}{20} \delta}{\frac{1}{3} \delta}, \frac{\frac{3}{20} \delta}{\frac{1}{3} \delta} \right)$$ Substitute.

$$(\bar{x}, \bar{y}) = \left(\frac{9}{20}, \frac{9}{20} \right) \qquad \frac{3}{20} \div \frac{1}{3} = \frac{3}{20} \cdot \frac{3}{1} = \frac{9}{20}$$

Note that for a planar lamina of uniform density, the density cancels out when finding the center of mass. The center of mass in this situation (uniform density) is also called the **centroid**.

EXAMPLE 29

Find the centroid of the region bounded by $f(x) = 3x - 2$ and $g(x) = x^2$.

SOLUTION 29

Return to Example 1 for a sketch of the region. The intersection points were (1, 1) and (2, 4).

$$M_x = \frac{1}{2} \int_1^2 [(3x-2)^2 - (x^2)^2] \, dx$$ Find M_x.

$$= \frac{1}{2} \int_1^2 (9x^2 - 12x + 4 - x^4) \, dx$$ Simplify.

$$= \frac{1}{2} \left[3x^3 - 6x^2 + 4x - \frac{1}{5} x^5 \right] \Big|_1^2$$ Integrate.

$$= \frac{1}{2} \left[(3(2)^3 - 6(2)^2 + 4(2) - \frac{1}{5}(2)^5) \right.$$

$$- \left(3(1)^3 - 6(1)^2 + 4(1) - \frac{1}{5}(1)^5\right)\Bigg]$$

$$= \frac{1}{2}\left[\frac{4}{5}\right] = \frac{2}{5}$$

$$M_y = \int_1^2 x[(3x-2) - x^2]\, dx \qquad\qquad \text{Find } M_y.$$

$$= \int_1^2 (3x^2 - 2x - x^3)\, dx \qquad\qquad \text{Simplify.}$$

$$= \left[x^3 - x^2 - \frac{x^4}{4}\right]\Bigg|_1^2 \qquad\qquad \text{Integrate.}$$

$$= \left[\left((2)^3 - (2)^2 - \frac{(2)^4}{4}\right) - \left(1^3 - 1^2 - \frac{1^4}{4}\right)\right]$$
$$\text{Evaluate.}$$

$$= \frac{1}{4} \qquad\qquad\qquad\qquad \text{Simplify.}$$

Finding the mass is equivalent to finding the area,

$$\int_1^2 [f(x) - g(x)]\, dx = \frac{1}{6}$$

(from Example 1.) Thus,

$$(\bar{x}, \bar{y}) = \left(\frac{M_y}{m}, \frac{M_x}{m}\right)$$

$$= \left(\frac{\frac{1}{4}}{\frac{1}{6}}, \frac{\frac{2}{5}}{\frac{1}{6}}\right)$$

$$= \left(\frac{3}{2}, \frac{12}{5}\right)$$

*T*his chapter presented a few applications of integration. A sketch of the given situation was useful in setting up solutions to the applications we studied. A summary of the formulas we used in the chapter follows.

Area between curves

$$A = \int_a^b [f(x) - g(x)] \, dx$$

Volume using the disc method

$$V = \pi \int_{x_1}^{x_2} [f(x)]^2 \, dx$$

or

$$V = \pi \int_{y_1}^{y_2} [g(y)]^2 \, dy$$

Volume using the washer method

$$V = \pi \int_{x_1}^{x^2} [(R(y))^2 - (r(x))^2] \, dx$$

or

$$V = \pi \int_{y_1}^{y_2} [(R(x))^2 - (r(y))^2] \, dy$$

Volume by shells

$$V = 2\pi \int_{x_1}^{x_2} r(x) \, h(x) \, dx$$

or

$$V = 2\pi \int_{y_1}^{y_2} r(y) \, h(y) \, dy$$

Length of a curve

$$L = \int_a^b \sqrt{1 + [f'(x)]^2}\, dx$$

or

$$L = \int_c^d \sqrt{1 + [g'(y)]^2}\, dy$$

Surface area

$$S = 2\pi \int_a^b \left(r(x) \sqrt{1 + [f'(x)]^2} \right) dx$$

or

$$S = 2\pi \int_c^d \left(r(y) \sqrt{1 + [g'(y)]^2} \right) dy$$

Work

$$W = \int_a^b F(x)\, dx$$

Fluid force

$$F = \delta \int_{y_1}^{y_2} h \cdot L\, dy$$

Moment about the x-axis

$$M_x = \frac{\delta}{2} \int_a^b [f^2(x) - g^2(x)]\, dx$$

Moment about the y-axis

$$M_y = \delta \int_a^b x\, [f(x) - g(x)]\, dx$$

Center of mass

$$(\bar{x}, \bar{y}) = (\frac{M_y}{m}, \frac{M_x}{m})$$

where

$$m = \delta \int_{a}^{b} [f(x) - g(x)] \, dx$$

Practice Exercises

1. Find the area bounded by $f(x) = \frac{1}{2}x^2$ and $g(x) = -\frac{1}{2}x + 3$.

2. Find the area bounded by $2x - y = 3$ and $x = \frac{1}{3}y^2$.

3. Find the area bounded by $f(x) = x^3 - x$ and $g(x) = 3x$

4. Find the volume of the solid formed by revolving the region bounded by $f(x) = 1 - x^2$, $x = 0$, $y = 0$, about the x-axis.

5. Find the volume of the solid formed by revolving the region bounded by $f(x) = 1 - x^2$, $x = 0$, $y = 0$, about the y-axis.

6. Find the volume of the solid formed by revolving the region bounded by $f(x) = 1 - x^2$, $y = \frac{1}{2}$, $x = 0$, about $y = \frac{1}{2}$.

7. Find the volume of the solid formed by revolving the region bounded by $f(x) = 1 - x^2$, $y = 1/2$, $x = 0$, about the x-axis.

8. Find the volume of the solid of revolution formed by revolving the region bounded by $y = x^3 + 3$, $x = 1$, $x = 0$, and $y = 0$ about $x = 0$.

9. Find the volume of the solid of revolution formed by revolving the region bounded by $y = x^3 + 3$, $x = 1$, $x = 0$, and $y = 0$ about $x = 1$.

10. Find the volume of the solid of revolution formed by revolving the region bounded by $y = x^3$, $x = 0$, $y = 1$ about the line $y = 2$.

11. Find the arc length of $f(x) = \frac{1}{2}x^{3/2} - 1$ on $[0, 1]$.

12. Find the arc length of $f(x) = 4x + 2$ on $[1, 3]$. (Check this using the distance formula.)

13. Find the arc length of $f(x) = \frac{1}{6}x^3 + \frac{1}{2x}$ on $[1, 2]$.

14. Set up the definite integral that represents the arc length of $y = \cos x$ on $[0, \pi]$.

15. Find the area of the surface formed by revolving $f(x) = 4x + 2$ on $[1, 3]$ about the x-axis.

16. Find the area of the surface formed by revolving the region bounded by $x = 4\sqrt{y}$, $0 \le y \le 4$ about the y-axis.

17. Find the work done to lift 100 pounds 5 feet.

18. A force of 20 pounds compresses a spring 4 inches from its natural length of 12 inches. Find the work done in compressing the spring a total of 8 inches.

19. A force of 8 kilograms stretches a spring 4.6 centimeters. How much work must be done to stretch the spring an additional 3 centimeters?

20. A cylindrical tank of diameter 12 feet and height of 15 feet is filled with water. Find the work done to pump the water over the top edge of the tank.

21. A cylindrical tank of diameter 12 feet and height of 15 feet is filled with liquid weighing 24 lb/ft^3. Find the work done to pump the liquid 1 foot above the top of the tank.

22. The vertical end of a tank filled with water has the shape of a rectangle as shown below. If the depth of the water is 5 feet, find the total force against the end of the tank. Use $\delta = 62.4$ pounds per cubic foot.

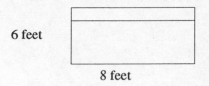

6 feet   8 feet

23. Find the fluid force on the given vertical plate submerged in water.

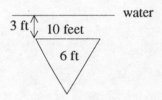

water
3 ft   10 feet
6 ft

24. A swimming pool is 10 feet wide, 75 feet long, 3 feet deep at one end and 6 feet deep at the other end. Find the fluid force against one of the 75 foot walls when the pool is filled with water.

25. Find the center of mass for a system with $m_1 = 8$ at $x_1 = 4$, $m_2 = 5$ at $x_2 = -1$, $m_3 = 12$ at $x_3 = -4$.

26. Find the center of mass for a system with $m_1 = 10$ at $(3, 4)$, $m_2 = 4$ at $(-1, -6)$, $m_3 = 5$ at $(2, -4)$ and $m_4 = 1$ at $(-2, 3)$.

27. Find the moments and the center of mass for the planar lamina of density δ bounded by $f(x) = x + 6$ and $g(x) = x^2$.

Answers

1. $\dfrac{125}{12}$

2. $\dfrac{81}{16}$

3. 8

4. $\dfrac{8}{15}\pi$

5. $\dfrac{1}{2}\pi$

6. $\dfrac{\sqrt{2}}{15}\pi$

7. $\dfrac{7\pi\sqrt{2}}{30}$

8. $\dfrac{17\pi}{5}$

9. $\dfrac{31\pi}{10}$

10. $\dfrac{15\pi}{7}$

11. $\dfrac{61}{54}$

12. $2\sqrt{17}$

13. $\dfrac{17}{12}$

14. $\displaystyle\int_{0}^{\pi}\sqrt{\sin^2 x + 1}\,dx$

15. $40\pi\sqrt{17}$

16. $\dfrac{16\pi}{3}[8^{3/2} - 8]$

17. 500 ft $\cdot$ lb

18. 160 inch pounds

19. Approximately 31.8 cm $\cdot$ kg

20. $252{,}720\pi$ ft $\cdot$ lb or approximately $793{,}943$ ft $\cdot$ lb

21. $110{,}160\pi$ ft $\cdot$ lb or approximately $346{,}078$ ft $\cdot$ lb

22. 8736 pounds

23. 9360 pounds

24. $49{,}140$ pounds

25. $-\dfrac{21}{25}$

26. $(\dfrac{17}{10}, -\dfrac{1}{20})$

27. $M_x = \dfrac{250}{3}\delta$

   $M_y = \dfrac{125}{12}\delta$

   $(\bar{x}, \bar{y}) = (\dfrac{1}{2}, 5)$

Index